Simply Amazing
Quilted Photography™

Learn everything you need to transform fabric into photographs

Tammie Bowser

◆ Bowser Publications/Mosaic Quilt Studio, South Pasadena, California

Simply Amazing
Quilted Photography ™

Learn everything you need to transform fabric into photographs

By Tammie Bowser

Attention Teachers:
Bowser Publications encourages you to use this book as a text for teaching. Contact us at www.QuiltedPhoto.com or at 626-799-5998 for more information about our teacher support program.

Library of Congress Cataloging in Publication Data
Bowser, Tammie
      Simply amazing quilted photography / Tammie Bowser
      ISBN 1-887467-60-2 (paper trade)
      1. Quilting. 2. Quilting--Art.
      3. Quilting--Patterns.
      I. Title.
Library of Congress Control Number: 2002094459

Published by:
      Bowser Publications
      917 Fremont, PMB138
      South Pasadena, California 91030

Printed in the U.S.A.

Table Of Contents

◆ ◆

Acknowledgments

Even though I have spent many days at my sewing machine and many long nights at my computer, I did not create this book all by myself. I could never have finished it without the love and support of a few people.

I would like to thank each of them here. First of all, I want to thank God for giving me wonderful creativity and an endless source of ideas. To my daughter Angela, thank you for loving me, inspiring me, and reminding me of the most important things in life. Alma, for providing a magical, comfortable place for Angela to play while I was working. Lori, thank you for taking the time out of your busy schedule to take the beautiful photos of my quilts! Grandaddy, thank you for your endless enthusiasm and for traveling so far just to help me. Thank you mom for being my editor, and for being my biggest fan from the beginning!

I love you all and I could not have done it without you!

Tammie

Preface

The goal of this book is to teach you how to make your own Quilted Photos. When you first look at the pictures of the finished Quilted Photos, your natural assumption will be that they are hard to make. The process is easy, and also fast! The truth is, the process is very easy to do if you take the time to understand each step, one at a time. My suggestion is that you read the book completely before starting any of the Quilted Photo projects.

Making a Quilted Photo is a weekend project! The Quilted Photo patterns in this book are beginner projects and believe it or not I am a beginning quilter. The step by step instructions explain the simple concepts you need to understand. Read each chapter one at a time to really understand the simple concepts and your Quilted Photo projects will always be successful.

Since quilted photography is fast and easy, it is a great way to get young people interested in sewing and quilting. One fourteen year old student took my (6 hour) class and won a blue ribbon with her quilt at the Los Angeles County Fair in the summer of 2002.

"The best pictures, and, from a technical point of view, the most complete, seen from near by, are but patches of color side by side, and only make an effect at a certain distance." These are the words of Vincent Van Gogh stated in November of 1885. This statement was true in 1885, and it is still true in 2003.

Quilted Photos can preserve your cherished family photos and transform them into works of art. I hope you will become as amazed with Quilted Photography as I am. Thank you for your interest in "Simply Amazing Quilted Photography" and thank you for purchasing this book.

If you have any comments or questions that are not answered in the following instructions, please go to my website to ask me personally: www.QuiltedPhoto.com

Understanding Quilted Photography

In this chapter

◆ Why Do The Fabrics Look Like A Photo?
◆ Tools And Materials You Will Need

Why do the fabrics look like a photo?

While studying graphic design, and computers I discovered that computerized photographs are not really photographs at all, they are just small squares of color that are arranged in a way that causes you to see an image. The more squares that are used to create the image, the clearer the image appears.

This concept works for fabric, tile or anything you can think of. It also works if the squares of color are dots, stars, triangles or any other shape. If you want to test this theory just find any book, newspaper or magazine, and examine a photograph with a magnifying glass. You will see small dots of color.

If you have already looked at the Quilted Photos in chapter 7, you probably are wondering why it is possible to use colors like blue, and purple and orange for a face? The colors are so unrealistic, yet the photograph is so real. Well that is because color value is much more important than just color alone. Color value is how light or dark a color is in relation to the other fabrics surrounding it. In chapter 2, I will show you how to sort your fabrics by color value. This special process will enable you to make a black and white image using colored fabrics!

Humans can see millions of colors, and most of the printed photographs you see in books, and magazines have hundreds of colors and shades in them. It would be a nightmare to manage a quilting project that has hundreds of different fabrics!

I have experimented with different numbers of fabrics. The number of fabrics that I have found to be manageable is 24. This number of fabrics will make your Quilted Photo projects beautiful, and intriguing!

Tools and Materials You Will Need

I will list all of the tools and materials you will need to make a quilted photograph. Each item is followed by a description of the item and how it is used.

Fusible Interfacing

Fusible interfacing is a very thin kind of fabric that has an adhesive on one side. The adhesive is activated when heat is applied with an iron. You will use the fusible interfacing to hold all of your fabric squares in place.

There are two types of fusible interfacing you can use, plain and pre-printed. You will find out more details about choosing interfacing in chapter 4.

Grid Guide

A grid guide is a large piece of paper that has a printed grid on it. The grid guide is placed under your plain fusible interfacing as a guide for placing your fabric squares. A grid guide can be used over and over to create photo quilts. I have included a grid guide with this book, but you can also get them at my website.

Fabrics For Quilt Top

I make my quilts with 24 fabrics, this amount creates an interesting mix of fabrics to look at. You will need one quarter yard or less of each fabric. This is a great way to make something really beautiful out of your scraps or your collection of fat quarters. Read chapter 2 to find out about choosing colors and fabrics.

Neutral Color Thread

Since you will be using 24 different fabrics ranging from light to dark, you will need a neutral, medium colored thread to stitch the squares together. Use 100% cotton or poly/cotton thread.

Clear Quilting Thread

After the quilt top is finished, you will need clear quilting thread to stitch the quilting. You will need clear thread because you cannot match all 24 fabrics with one color thread. You can find clear quilting thread at your local quilting shop.

Batting

Batting is the filler in the center of the quilt. Batting is widely available in polyester, poly/cotton blends and 100% cotton. I prefer 100% cotton batting because it is flat when it is quilted, but use what you prefer. You should be able to find batting at most fabric and craft stores as well as quilting shops.

Fabric For Backing and Binding

You will need to use a fabric for the back of the quilt as well as the binding around the edges of the quilt. I usually use more of one of the fabric in the quilt, but you can choose any fabric you like. For the binding, I have found that it is best to use a darker color, because the binding acts as a frame for your quilted image.

Small Scissors

You will need a small pair of scissors with very sharp points. The scissors are used to clip lots of little seams. The scissors I use have a spring in the handle which makes them very easy to use.

Fabric Organizer

The fabric organizer is used to keep all your fabric squares neat and organized. It has 24 compartments of the perfect size. Look at chapter 3 to see just how important this simple tool is. You can find them at www.QuiltedPhoto.com.

Basting Spray

The basting spray is a spray adhesive that holds the quilt top, the batting and backing together. The basting spray is an optional item, but I like it because it eliminates the step of basting the three quilt layers together by hand. You should be able to find it at your local quilt shop. It is a great time saver!

Fine Sewing Machine Needles

Fine sewing machine needles are another optional item, but they are good to use because the holes created in the fabric while stitching your fabrics together are almost invisible.

Distance Viewer

This is my favorite tool! This small scope will let you easily see the photographic image in your quilt, even close up! It is useful while you are working on the quilt, and it is fun to use after the quilt is finished. Each time I work on a new quilt, I think to myself "It didn't work this time", then I look at the quilt through the distance viewer, and the image just pops out at me! If you plan to make any of these quilts as gifts, you must give them a distance viewer too! You can get Distance Viewers at, www.QuiltedPhoto.com

Iron

An iron is needed to fuse the fabric squares onto the fusible interfacing. You can use your household iron, but if you plan to make more of these quilts I recommend that you get an inexpensive iron dedicated just to Quilted Photography.

Rotary Cutter

A rotary cutter is a specialized cutting tool that is useful for cutting small fabric shapes. You will need a rotary cutter with a nice sharp blade. The blade needs to be sharp so that you can cut accurate fabric squares. Rotary cutters are available in most fabric and quilt shops.

Long Ruler with Handle

You will need a ruler that is about 24" long and 6" wide. The ruler also needs a lip to help you quickly cut accurate squares. You will also need a handle that attaches to your ruler. Read chapter 3 to learn how to use the ruler (with a lip, and handle) to quickly cut the squares. Stop by my website to get your own.

Cutting Mat

You will need a cutting mat to protect your table from the rotary cutter blade. It will need to be at least 18" x 24" in size. You can find cutting mats at most fabric and quilt shops. Come to my website to see the special cutting mat that I use.

Sewing Machine

Your sewing machine should be in good working order, and have a ¼" seam allowance clearly marked.

Walking or Free Motion Quilting Foot

These items are optional but helpful for machine quilting. Refer to the documentation for your sewing machine for availability of parts and how to use them.

Flat Work Surface

You will need a large flat work surface for placing the squares. This surface can be a dining table or any other table that is a comfortable height to stand at. If you use a dining table, you might want to cover it with an inexpensive cardboard cutting mat to protect the surface. Cardboard cutting mats are easy to find at the large chain fabric stores.

Photocopy machine
You don't have to own a copy machine, but you will need to have access to one. Make a black and white copy of all of your fabrics to determine the color value of each fabric. See chapter 2 to understand more about color value, and its importance.

UV Protection Spray
This spray is optional but I highly recommend it! This spray acts as a sunscreen for your finished quilted masterpiece! If you use this spray, the sun won't fade the colors in your quilt. Ask for UV protection spray at your local quilt shop.

Choosing Fabrics & Colors

In this chapter

◆ What Is Color Value?
◆ The 8-8-8 Rule
◆ Choosing The Color Palette
◆ How To Choose Prints
◆ Color Value Photocopy Forms

What Is Color Value?

Color value is how light or dark a fabric is in relation to the other fabrics in your color palette. A color palette is the collection of fabrics used to make your quilt. The most important step in making a quilted photo is arranging your 24 fabrics in order (from light to dark) by color value. I have found that it is hard for me to see the color value of fabrics with my naked eyes. My eyes are easily fooled by the colors. To solve this problem, I use a process that allows me to see the values of the fabrics separately from the colors.

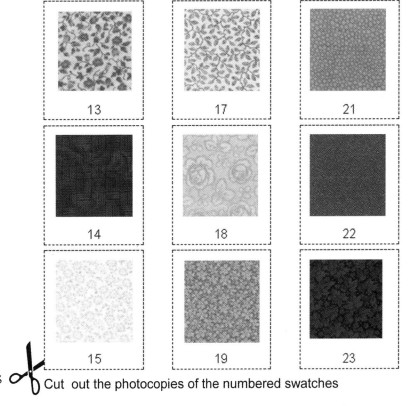

 Cut out the photocopies of the numbered swatches

Finding The Value Of Fabrics

Cut a small piece of the fabrics you will be using to make your quilted photo. Photocopy the forms at the end of this chapter, then tape one fabric piece in each of the boxes. Make a black and white photocopy of the fabrics. The photocopy will erase the colors, and only show you the value. Cut the photocopied swatches apart, and arrange them in order from light to dark. Now it will be very easy to see the correct order of the swatches. If two of your swatches look like they have the same color value, then make your decision about which fabric is lighter and which

is darker by looking at the colors. You will use the numbers on the form to identify the fabric order. Place your sorted swatches in a plastic organizer box (read more about organizing your fabrics in chapter 3).

Once you have your fabrics in order by color value, your success is guaranteed! Not only is color value very important but it is even more important than the colors you choose! If you follow the instructions above to sort your fabrics, you will effortlessly create highlights, shadows, and depth in your quilted photograph.

Photocopied fabrics sorted by color value

| 15 | 18 | 17 | 13 | 19 | 21 | 22 | 14 | 23 |

The 8-8-8 Rule

Another helpful guideline I use when choosing my fabrics is what I call the 8-8-8 Rule. You must have 8 light colored fabrics, 8 medium colored fabrics, and 8 dark colored fabrics.

Your goal is to have colored fabrics that represent shades from white to black. Don't be afraid to pick really light shades, as well as really dark shades. You should be able to easily follow the 8-8-8 Rule while choosing your fabrics.

Do not worry about putting the fabrics in the exact order by color value yet, you'll be able to do that later, just concentrate on the 8-8-8 Rule while selecting your fabrics.

Choosing The Color Palette

A color palette is a collection of fabrics chosen for a quilted photo project. Choosing the colors for your quilted image is the most creative part of the whole process! Your photograph will become art with your selection of colors. Andy Warhol was a famous artist who is known for manipulating the colors of popular photographs and images. You will essentially be doing the same thing.

While shopping for your fabric, you may choose any colors you like but your choices will determine the final look of your quilt photo. For example your quilt will have a sophisticated look if you choose muted colors or neutral shades as your color palette. If you select primary colors, or very bright colors, your quilt will have a lively, fun look.

Most of the time, when I choose my color palettes I choose from my personal collection of fabrics. I usually don't go on a special shopping trip for each project. My collection of fabric is made up of fabrics I like, so I always like the finished quilts. If you have been quilting for any length of time you probably have a collection of fabrics that you love right at your fingertips as well! There are several ways you can choose your colors (one or all of the ways may surprise you)! I will explain each of them.

Restricted color palette

A restricted color palette is a very restricted range of color. This range can have as few as 2 colors as shown in the quilt of Emily on page 67. While choosing your fabrics, be sure to observe the 8-8-8 rule. The color palette for the Emily quilt was made of the colors pink and purple (because these are Emily's favorite colors). A restricted color palette is great for faces, or hands.

Random color palette

A random color palette is made up of fabrics of any color combination. Choosing your color palette at random is fun! I call a quilted photo made with a random color palette the ultimate scrap quilt! The random color palette is the most surprising type of palette. It really is hard to believe that putting 24 totally beautiful photographic quilt. You could even use all of your favorite fabrics, just be sure to follow the 8-8-8 Rule. Once you make a photo quilt with a random color palette, you will understand the importance of color value once and for all. The quilted image of Lauren on page 69 is very beautiful, and was made with a random color palette. If you have a hard time deciding on what colors and fabrics to use for your quilt projects, then try a random color palette. You will not have to make any hard fabric selection decisions; you will only have the 8-8-8 Rule to remember. A random color palette is great for faces, or hands.

Single color palette
A single color palette is made up of just one color, from the lightest to the darkest shades. This type of palette will work well with any image. It will be like making a colorized black and white photo. Just remember to follow the 8-8-8 Rule while choosing the single color palette. You can see an example of a single color palette in the Money quilt on page 61.

Realistic color palette
A realistic color palette is made up of fabric that closely resemble the colors of the original photograph. Choosing the fabrics for a realistic color palette is the most challenging type of palette to put together. It is more challenging because you will have to consider the colors and values of the fabrics at the same time. This could mean you will have to shop around to find just the right fabrics to match the color palette provided with each pattern. A realistic color palette is always very impressive, and you can see an example of this type of quilt on page 62 called "Cherubs".

How To Choose Prints
I really love using printed fabrics for my photo quilts. They give my quilts a complex look without adding to the difficulty of the quilt project. There are 2 important rules for using prints.

Rule #1
Only use prints that are medium or small in scale. Large prints are not suitable because the color value can change.

Rule #2
Try to avoid prints that have a background that is too highly contrasted. For example a white dot, with a black background would not be suitable because you will not be able to decide on the correct color value. Example A shows a hard to use fabric. Example B is a better choice.

Example A

Example B

Color Value Photocopy Form

First photocopy these forms, then attach your fabric swatches to the squares with tape or glue. Cut out the photocopied swatches. Arrange them in order by color value.

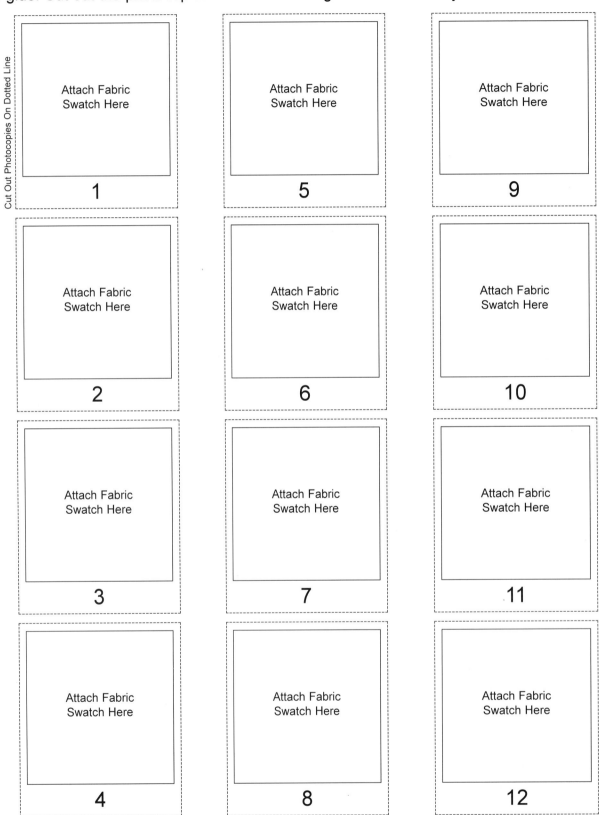

Color Value Photocopy Form

Attach Fabric Swatch Here 13	Attach Fabric Swatch Here 17	Attach Fabric Swatch Here 21
Attach Fabric Swatch Here 14	Attach Fabric Swatch Here 18	Attach Fabric Swatch Here 22
Attach Fabric Swatch Here 15	Attach Fabric Swatch Here 19	Attach Fabric Swatch Here 23
Attach Fabric Swatch Here 16	Attach Fabric Swatch Here 20	Attach Fabric Swatch Here 24

"What impassions me most--
much, much more than all the
rest of my me'tier-- is the
portrait, the modern portrait."

Vincent Van Gogh, June1890

How To Prepare The Fabric

In this chapter

◆ The Size Of The Squares
◆ Quick Cutting Tips
◆ Swatch Organization

The Size Of The Squares

Now you must cut your fabric. You can choose any size squares you like. The size of the square you decide to use, will determine the final size of your quilt. The size of the squares will also determine how much fabric you will need. The size of the squares will also determine how far away from the quilt you will need to stand to see the image. With these things in mind, we do have a few recommendations to help you choose your square size.

The size of the square you use is very important. For example a quilt I made with 1½" squares finished 24"x40". The same quilt made with 1" squares will only be 12"x20" and if it were made with 2" squares, the quilt would be 36"x60". Notice how the size of the quilt changes with each different square size.

The other thing you must consider while choosing the square size is where the quilt will be displayed when it is finished. The size of the square will determine the distance that will be required to see the photo image. The bigger squares require more distance, and the smaller squares will need less distance. The magical beauty of these photo quilts is that when you

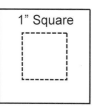

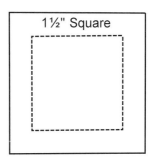

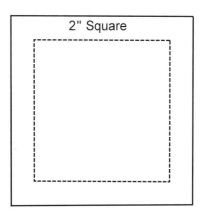

look at the quilt from a distance you will see the photo very clearly, but as you get closer to the quilt, the image will disappear right before your eyes! When you are standing close to your quilt you will only see a beautiful mosaic of fabrics.

I like working with 1¼" squares. This size is easy to work with, and the size of the quilt top before stitching the seams will be manageable. A quilt with a larger square size will be great for a large display area where it can be viewed at an appropriate distance. If you make a photo quilt with 2" squares, and you do not have an appropriate place to display it, you will not be able to view the image clearly.I have found that using 1¼" squares strikes just the right balance of manageability while sewing, reasonable viewing distance, and a square size that is not to big or to small.

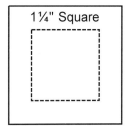

1¼" Square

Quick Cutting Tips

To begin cutting your fabric I recommend that you use a rotary cutter, ruler and mat. When you cut your fabric please use all the safety precautions, and methods described by the manufacturers of the equipment.

I use a special ruler with a lip on the edge that makes cutting accurate squares very easy. The lip guide keeps the ruler perfectly straight while cutting.

I also use a handle on my ruler. The handle allows me to apply pressure to the layers of fabric. The applied pressure keeps the fabrics from moving while cutting. To learn about this special ruler and accessories, please go to my website for more information.

To Begin Your Cutting
1. First fold your fabric in half with the salvage edges of the fabric together as shown.

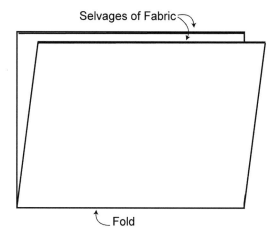

Selvages of Fabric

Fold

2. Now fold the fabric in half again matching the salvage edges to the folded edge.

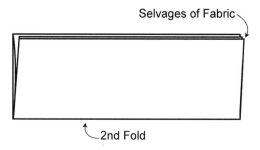

Selvages of Fabric

2nd Fold

3. Using your rotary cutter and mat, cut strips the width of your desired square size. To make accurate squares, I use the guidelines on the cutting mat as well as the lines on the ruler.

4. Place the folded edge of the fabric on a guideline on the cutting mat as shown. Now if your ruler has a lip on the bottom, you will be able to slide it along the straight edge of the cutting mat to help you cut with accuracy. This process will go quickly once you get the hang of it.

Use a rotary cutter and mat to cut strips the width of your squares

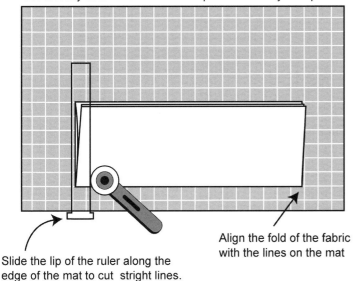

Slide the lip of the ruler along the edge of the mat to cut stright lines.

Align the fold of the fabric with the lines on the mat

5. Once you cut the strips, place them horizontally on the cutting mat, following the lines of the cutting mat. Now slide the ruler along the edge of the mat to cut your strips into squares.

Align the folds of the strips with the lines on the mat

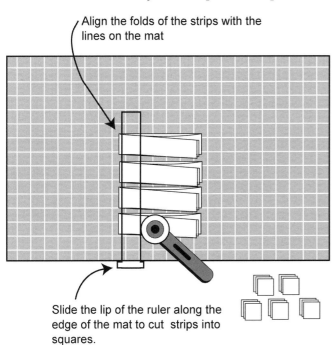

Slide the lip of the ruler along the edge of the mat to cut strips into squares.

The fabric squares will be referred to as swatches for the remainder of the book.

Swatch Organization

After you have cut all your fabrics, make sure to place them in order from light to dark in your fabric organizer. Then number them from 1-24 with #1 being the lightest color. This organizer box will prevent you from losing any swatches, and it will also keep the fabrics labeled. To label the compartments, just use a permanent marker to write the number directly in each of the spaces.

What if I run out of a fabric?

If you miscalculate your yardage needs and run out of a fabric you can substitute with another fabric. Since the quilt has so many fabrics no one will ever notice the substitution. The rule for substituting fabrics is it has to have a color value that is darker than the fabric before it, and lighter in value than the fabric after it.

"The best pictures, and, from a technical point of view, the most complete, seen from near by, are but patches of color side by side, and only make an effect at a certain distance."

Vincent Van Gogh, November 1885

How To Put The Quilt Together

In this chapter.

- ◆ How To Read The Patterns
- ◆ About Fusible Interfacings
- ◆ What Is A Grid Guide?
- ◆ Placing the Swatches
- ◆ Sewing The Seams

How To Read The Patterns

If you look at the patterns in this book, the pattern information is stored in a grid. You have three options for using the patterns. 1) purchase gridded, fusible interfacing to layout fabric swatches, 2) use a paper grid guide (we have included a grid guide with this book) to place under your plain fusible interfacing, or 3) draw your own grid guide with a large sheet of paper and a pen. You'll learn more about Grid Guides later in this chapter.

About Fusible Interfacings

Fusible interfacing is a very thin kind of fabric that has an adhesive on one side. The adhesive is activated when heat is applied with an iron. You will use the fusible interfacing to hold all of your fabric swatches in place.

Gridded Fusible Interfacing

This is fusible interfacing with a grid printed directly on one side. You can purchase gridded fusible interfacings at your local fabric store or quilt shop. The gridded fusible interfacing comes in panels, or running yardage that is either 44/45" or 60" wide. The most common grid sizes are 1", 1 ½", and 2". You can use any of these grid sizes, but re-read "The Size Of The Squares" on page 17 before you decide what size to use.

Before using any of the gridded interfacings, read the manufacturer's instructions very carefully. The adhesives that are used are sensitive and may not stick well if the instructions are not followed correctly. Just as a general rule I suggest that you test out the interfacing before you place all of the fabric swatches. You can test the fusible interfacing by ironing a fabric swatch to a small piece of the interfacing. You should use the iron setting you intend to use for your quilt project. Let the swatch and interfacing cool, then try to pull the swatch away from the interfacing to check if the adhesive is working well. If the swatch comes off easily, try it again at a different heat setting.

I have personally applied more heat to the gridded fusible interfacing (and some plain interfacings) then was recommended by the manufacturer, and my fabrics fell off! This is the worse thing that can happen while making a photo quilt project. Take my advice, test first and follow instructions.

Plain Fusible Interfacing

You can also use any lightweight fusible interfacing, but you will have to read the manufacturer's instructions very carefully before using.

I use plain fusible interfacing for all of my photo quilts. To use the plain fusible interfacing, you must also use a grid guide with it (included with this book). I have tested several and the best kind does not stretch much, you can see through it, it is applied with a dry iron, and has an adhesive that keeps the fabric swatches attached securely. Another good thing about this special interfacing is that you can pull off a swatch, and apply another and the adhesive will stick again! I have made this special fusible interfacing available at my website.

What Is A Grid Guide?

It is a printed grid that you place under the plain fusible interfacing as a guide for placement of your fabric swatches. The grid is printed on paper and you can use it again and again. The lightweight interfacings that are used to make photo quilts are so thin that you can easily see the guide through the interfacing. Also as an added bonus, you can transfer the pattern information directly to the grid guide with pencil, then erase and use it again. Just be sure to use a pencil with soft lead so that your numbers will erase easily.

Note: you can also transfer the pattern information to the gridded fusible interfacing but be careful to use a pen or pencil that will not stain your fabrics when you apply the iron.

Apply your swatches a section at a time, iron them in place then move on to the next section. Continue this process until the whole quilt top is complete. These guides are the perfect tools for using with the patterns in this book or other photo quilt projects you will want to make later.

You can make you own grid guides too. You will just need a pen, ruler and paper. The advantage to this is you can customize it for your own preferences. You will be able to choose any grid size, and you can make a guide that will fit your work surface perfectly. Be very careful to draw accurate grid lines. If you do not want to make your own grid guides, we have them available for sale at QuiltedPhoto.com.

Place your grid guide on your work surface, then place the fusible interfacing **sticky side up** on top of your grid guide. This is very important so I will say it again...**the adhesive side of the interfacing should be facing up, towards you!**

You will be able to see the grid and the numbers through the interfacing.

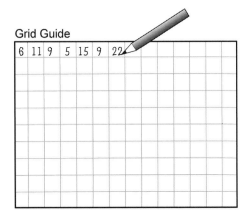

Grid Guide

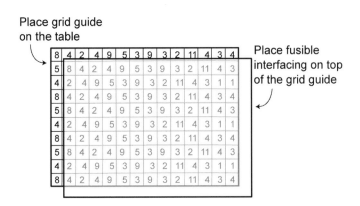

Place grid guide on the table

Place fusible interfacing on top of the grid guide

Placing The Swatches

Placing the fabric swatches is really fun because you will start to see the image emerge as you place more and more swatches.

Start placing your swatches on the interfacing following the pattern underneath.

After you finish placing the first section of swatches, iron the swatches in place. Transfer the next section of the pattern to your grid guide. Now align the grid guide with the swatches you've already applied to the interfacing, and continue with this process until the pattern is complete. You will see your photo image very soon! It usually takes me about 2 hours to put all of the swatches in place.

The correct way to iron the swatches is to pick the iron straight up, then put is straight down. Never slide the iron around on the surface of the quilt top before the swatches are secured to the fusible interfacing.

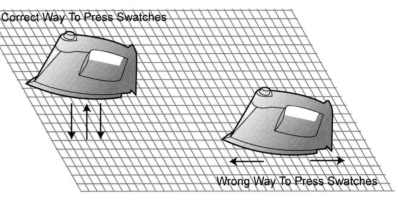

Correct Way To Press Swatches

Wrong Way To Press Swatches

To iron the swatches, put an ironing board right next to your work surface. Adjust the ironing board to the same height as the table. Gently pull the interfacing and swatches on to the ironing board and iron according to the interfacing manufacturer's instructions. Take care to iron the swatches with out moving them. Also try to avoid letting the hot iron touch the bare interfacing. Continue pressing a section at a time until the whole quilt top is fused in place. See the diagram on the next page.

Now is a good time to clean your iron. No matter how hard you try, you will get some of the adhesive on your iron. Clean it with a cotton cloth by wiping the plate while the iron is still really hot.

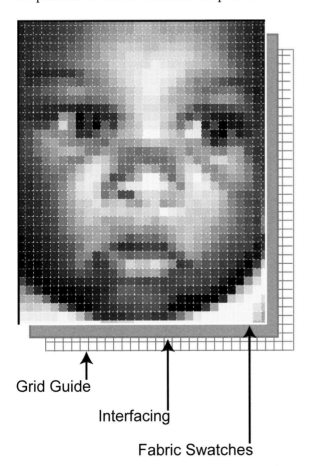

Grid Guide

Interfacing

Fabric Swatches

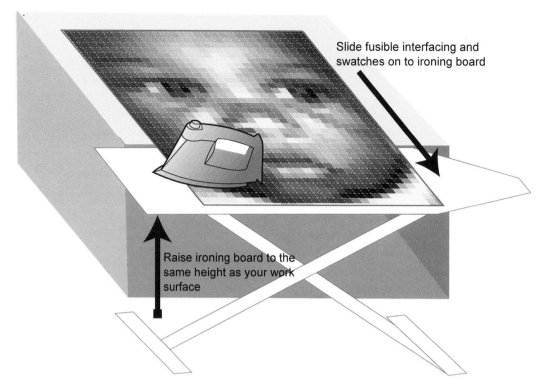

Slide fusible interfacing and swatches on to ironing board

Raise ironing board to the same height as your work surface

Remember that you will be working very close to your quilt and the images are best viewed at a distance. For every one of the quilts that I have made, I think to myself "It Didn't Work This Time!". I have to remember to step away from it or look at it though a Distance Viewer. The Distance Viewer is like a small telescope that will enable you to see the quilt picture immediately. See the order form at the end of this book, or go to www.QuiltedPhoto.com for this item.

After the swatches are all in place, look at them through the Distance Viewer to see if you like the image. If you want to make any changes this is your last chance to do so. To make the change, carefully remove the swatch and fuse the new swatch in place.

If you are using gridded fusible interfacing, be very careful while removing swatches, the gridded fusible interfacing tears easily. The gridded interfacing

probably will not have any adhesive left to stick the new swatch, so you will have to pin the new swatches in place.

Sewing The Seams

Although I am not the inventor of the "fuse, fold, and stitch" sewing method I am about to explain, it has made creating quilted photos a thousand times easier! I have adapted the method for my quilted photo projects.

Now to sew the quilt top together I recommend that you use a ¼" seam allowance guide on your sewing machine. This is to make sure that you

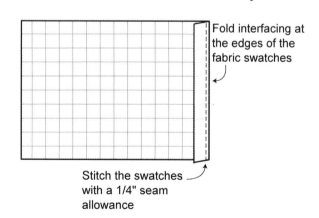

Fold interfacing at the edges of the fabric swatches

Stitch the swatches with a 1/4" seam allowance

maintain a consistent ¼" seam allowance throughout the project. Fold the quilt top along the edges of the squares, and stitch along all of the vertical rows of swatches. Iron the quilt top now to open up the seams before continuing with the horizontal rows of stitching.

Now with small sharp scissors, clip the intersection between each square.

Clip the seam allowances at each swatch intersection

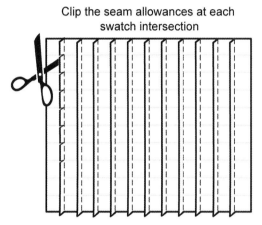

Clip all of the rows until every intersection is clipped. Do not be concerned about clipping the seams because the whole clipped intersection will be caught in the seam allowance for the horizontal seams.

Now to sew the horizontal rows, fold the seam allowances in opposite directions (as shown) so that the seams lock together. Staggering the seam allowances will distribute the bulk of the many seams. Continue stitching the staggered seams until all of the horizontal seams are finished.

Iron your quilt top carefully as not to distort the image.

Fold interfacing at the edges of the fabric swatches

Turn the seam allowances in opposite directions as shown.

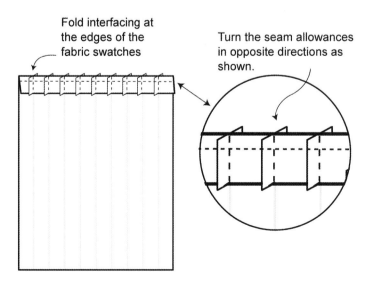

"I should like to paint portraits
which would appear after a century
to people living then as apparitions."

Vincent Van Gogh, June 1890

Finishing Your Quilt

In this chapter

Completing the project

Even though you have made your amazing photographic quilt top, the project is not complete until you have made it suitable for display. There are lots of ways for you to finish your quilt top. I will discuss each of the available options in this chapter. The options range from borders, to bindings, to stretching your quilt top like a canvas!

Trimming The Quilt

If you have sewn all of your seams with perfect seam allowances, your quilt will finish with perfectly straight edges and squared corners. However this never happens and it is o.k. if your quilt is not perfect because you can trim the edges of the quilt.

If you want to add a border to frame your quilt, trim the edges with your rotary cutter first. If you are just adding a binding to finish your quilt, then wait to trim the edges after stitching the layers of your quilt. Trimming will make sure that your quilt hangs straight when displayed on a wall.

The one thing you must do before trimming is carefully iron the quilt top.

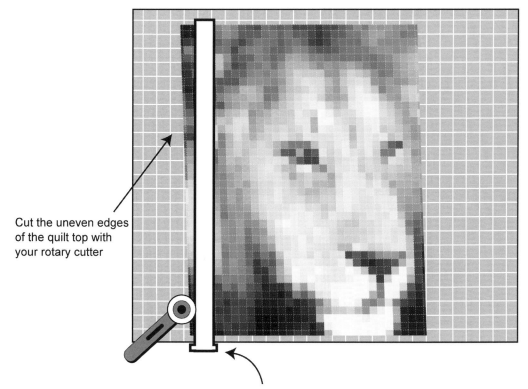

Cut the uneven edges of the quilt top with your rotary cutter

Slide the lip of the ruler along the edge of the mat to cut stright lines.

Adding Borders

A border is a straight strip of fabric sewn around the edges of your quilt to finish it.

A border can make your photo quilt even more beautiful but borders also have a practical purpose. Adding a border will make the edges of the quilt perfectly straight, and the corners will be perfectly squared. The border will make the quilted photo hang perfectly straight on the wall without any wavy edges. Another added bonus is the border will increase the size of the quilt and provide a place to put decorative quilting. Decorative quilting can not be seen very well on the quilt image, but you can add it effectively on a border.

Adding a border is a decision you will make after you see the finished quilt top. You can add one border, or two borders or no border at all.

When you think about adding borders to your quilted photos, you can pretend like you are adding a matting and frame. Pay attention to how paper photographs are framed. Also look at how paintings and other art work is finished for inspiration. Notice how the colors relate to the art work, and pay close attention to the proportion of the border in relation to the art work. There are two types of borders, straight cut borders and mitered borders. I will explain both types. To add a border, the first step is to measure at the center of the quilt in both directions. Be sure to

Diagram A - Straight Border

Diagram B - Mitered Border

measure in the center of the quilt because the edges of the quilt are probably stretched and are not accurate. The center measurements will determine what length to cut the border strips. Cut the borders strips across the width of the fabric.

Straight border

A straight border has straight seams on the corners. See diagram A on page 28. To add a straight border, the first step is to measure the center of the quilt horizontally. Cut two border strips this exact length. Stitch the borders to the sides of the quilt, easing the quilt top to match the border if it is necessary.

Next measure the center of the quilt in the vertical direction including the border that you just applied. Cut two border strips this exact length. Stitch the border to the quilt, easing the two together if it is necessary. If you want a second straight border, repeat this process.

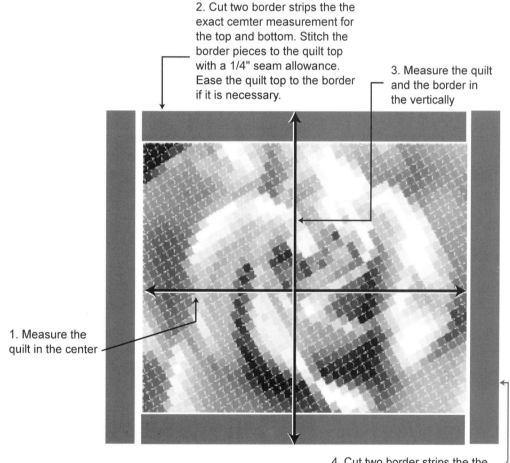

2. Cut two border strips the the exact cemter measurement for the top and bottom. Stitch the border pieces to the quilt top with a 1/4" seam allowance. Ease the quilt top to the border if it is necessary.

3. Measure the quilt and the border in the vertically

1. Measure the quilt in the center

4. Cut two border strips the the exact vertical measurement for each side of the quilt. Stitch the border pieces to the quilt top with a 1/4" seam allowance. Ease the quilt top to the border if it is necessary.

Mitered border

A mitered border is a border with diagonal seam on the corners. See diagram B on page 28.

To add a mitered border, first measure the center of the quilt in the vertical direction. Next measure the width of the border. Now cut two border strips the vertical length + the width of the border times 2. Mark the width of the border on each end of the border pieces. Cut the corners as shown in the diagram below. Cut from the outside corner, down to the border marks. Stitch the border pieces to the sides of the quilt, easing the quilt into the border if it is necessary. Stop your stitching ¼" from the edge. Repeat these steps for the horizontal edges of the quilt top.

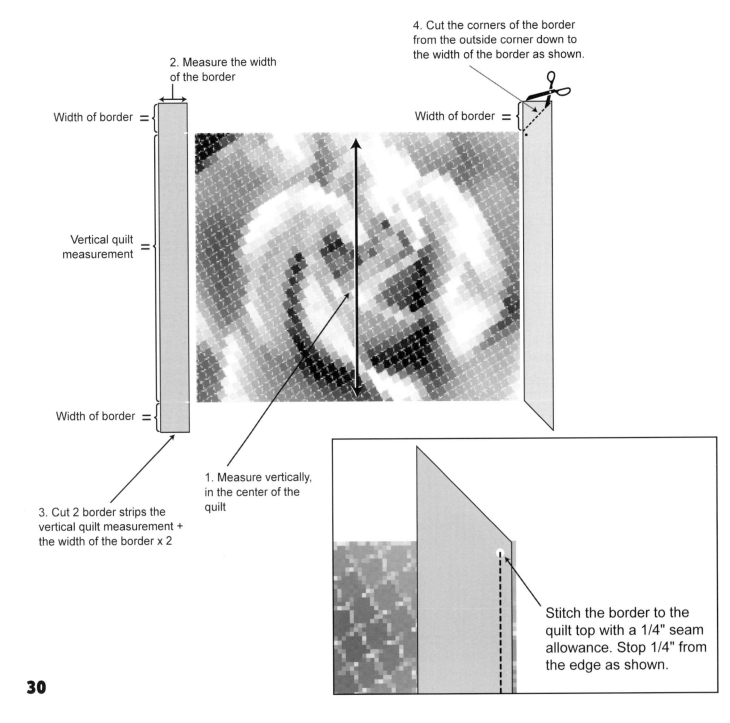

4. Cut the corners of the border from the outside corner down to the width of the border as shown.

2. Measure the width of the border

Width of border =

Width of border =

Vertical quilt measurement =

Width of border =

3. Cut 2 border strips the vertical quilt measurement + the width of the border x 2

1. Measure vertically, in the center of the quilt

Stitch the border to the quilt top with a 1/4" seam allowance. Stop 1/4" from the edge as shown.

To Create The Corner Seams

Fold the quilt in half diagonally so that the ends of the border meet. Stitch the corner seams with ¼" seam allowances. Repeat this step for all four corners.

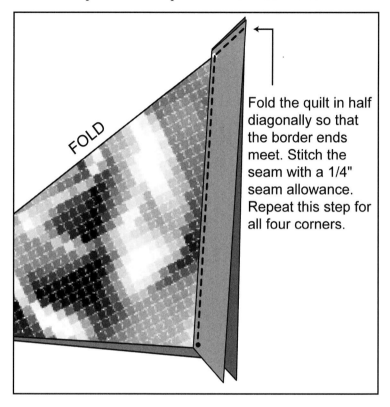

FOLD

Fold the quilt in half diagonally so that the border ends meet. Stitch the seam with a 1/4" seam allowance. Repeat this step for all four corners.

Batting And Backing

You can choose any backing fabric because the back of the quilt does not show. However I always use one of the fabrics that were used on the front of the quilt.

If your quilt top is larger than the width of the backing fabric, you will have to stitch two pieces of the backing fabric together to cover the back of the quilt. Remember to iron the backing seam open if a seam is required for your backing.

To sign your quilt, you can sign directly on the backing with a permanent pigment ink pen if you use a light colored fabric, or you can create an embroidered signature. You can also choose to apply a label to the back of the quilt.

The batting you use between the quilt top and the backing is again a matter of your preference. Batting is sold in standard bedding sizes as well as by the yard. Cotton battings are flatter when they are finished than polyester battings, but polyester and cotton blends are a good option as well. I usually use 100% cotton batting for my photo quilts. You can find batting in fabric and quilt stores.

Basting

Basting is a temporary bond that holds the quilt top, batting and backing together. Basting also assures that you will not have tucks or folds on the backing when you stich through your quilt sandwich.

You can baste the quilt sandwich by hand with a running stitch as shown in example A on page 32. Another option for basting is to use safety pins every few inches to smooth the layers of the quilt sandwich.

My favorite way to baste is to use an adhesive basting spray. Spray the adhesive between each layer of the quilt and the layers will hold together for the quilting process.See Example A on page32.

Basting stitched
through the
quilt sandwich

Quilt Top

Backing

Batting

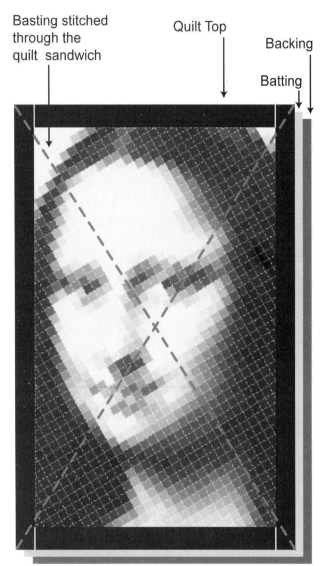

Example A

stitching is not decorative; it is to hold the quilt together smoothly. With this purpose in mind I suggest that you use a simple all over quilting pattern like a grid, stitching in the ditch, or a stipple pattern.

Simple Grid Quilting Pattern

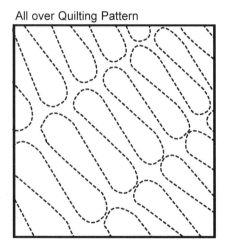

All over Quilting Pattern

Stipple Quilting Pattern

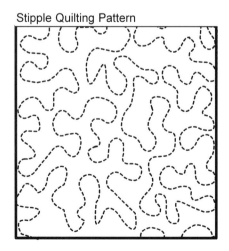

Quilting Suggestions

Your quilt will have many fabrics, many seams and will be very difficult to quilt by hand. For these reasons I suggest that you quilt by machine. Use clear thread for the top thread, and a thread that will match the backing for the bottom thread. You will need a free motion quilting foot, or a walking foot for machine quilting your quilt top.

The quilting pattern does not show because of the many fabrics used. If you quilted an intricate pattern, it would not be noticeable. The main purpose of the

If you do not like any of these quilting suggestions and you want to accent you quilt image more freely, try decorative threads and free motion quilting. This topic is beyond the scope of this book, look for another book about machine quilting for in depth instructions.

All over or Stipple Pattern

This is a continuous, curving stitch that never crosses over itself. To create this pattern beautifully, it takes practice but it is an excellent quilting pattern to use for any quilted photo project. Use a free motion quilting foot (with your sewing machine's feed dogs down) to create an all over stipple pattern.

Simple Grid Pattern

The simple grid is the easiest all over pattern for a quilted photo project. This pattern is vertical and horizontal lines of stitching arranged in a grid pattern. This pattern is easy to make because you use the corners of the fabric squares as guides for the straight rows of stitching. Use a walking foot to create the simple grid pattern.

Stitching In The Ditch

Stitching in the ditch is also grid patterned stitching. The difference between the simple grid, and stitching in the ditch is the stitching is hidden in the seams. The stitching should not show at all when using this quilting pattern. Stitching in the ditch is more difficult than the other patterns because mistakes are very visible. Use a walking foot to stitch in the ditch.

After the quilting is finished, you still need to finish the edges. You will finish the edges with a binding and I will show you how to make two different types.

Bindings

There are two types of bindings. The first type is a classic binding and the second type is an invisible binding.

Classic Binding

A classic binding will make a ¼" edge around the outside of the quilt. To make a classic binding, the first thing you will do is cut strips 1½" wide. Cut the strips across the width of the fabric. Stitch the strips together to form one long strip as shown in diagram A.

Diagram A

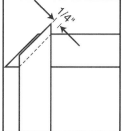

Fold the binding strip in half the long way, and then place the binding on the front of the quilt with the raw edges together. Stitch the binding with a ¼" seam allowance as shown in diagram B.

Diagram B

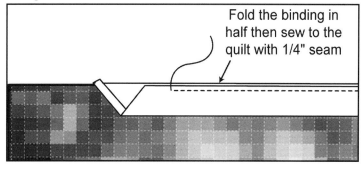

Fold the binding in half then sew to the quilt with 1/4" seam

To continue the binding around the corner, stop stitching ¼" from the edge.

Diagram C

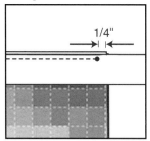

Fold the binding upward, creating an angled corner as shown in diagram D.

Diagram D

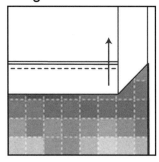

Then fold the binding back downward (creating a squared corner), leaving a fold of fabric as shown. Pin the fold in place and stitch the next side of the binding. You can begin stitching from the corner edge.

Diagram E

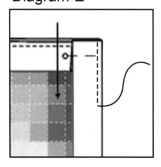

The next step is to wrap the binding around the quilt edge, then over to the back as shown in diagram F. The last step is to stitch the edge of the binding in place with a small whipstitch.

Diagram F

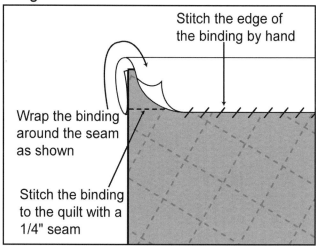

Stitch the edge of the binding by hand

Wrap the binding around the seam as shown

Stitch the binding to the quilt with a 1/4" seam

Invisible Binding

An invisible binding will not show at all when viewing the quilt from the front. To make an invisible binding, the first thing you will do is cut strips 1½" wide. Fold the binding strip in half, and then place the binding on the front of the quilt with the raw edges together. Stitch the binding with a ¼" seam allowance as shown in diagram B on page 33.

After stitching the binding all the way around the quilt, fold the binding and the seam upward, and away from the quilt. Stitch the binding 1/8" away from the seam as shown in the diagram below. This stitch will force the binding

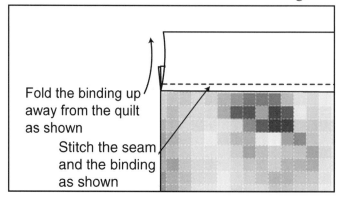

Fold the binding up away from the quilt as shown

Stitch the seam and the binding as shown

and the seam allowance to roll towards the backside of the quilt. The last step is to stitch the edge of the binding in place with a small whipstitch.

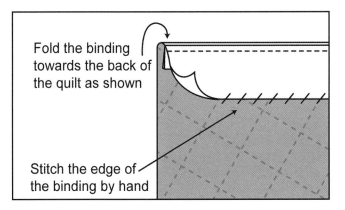

Fold the binding towards the back of the quilt as shown

Stitch the edge of the binding by hand

How To Display A Photo Quilt

When you prepare to display your quilt, you first need to think about how to care for the quilt. The most important thing you can do to preserve the quilt is to use UV protection spray. This spray will act just like a sunscreen and protect the fabrics from fading and sun damage.

Since these quilts are intended to be art that is hung on a wall, you should not have to worry about the quilts getting dirty. However you will need to remove dust from time to time if they are not framed behind glass. To remove the dust, just put the quilt in a clothes dryer for 10 minutes. The dryer will remove the dust without damaging the quilt.

After you have learned how to care for your quilt, you must decide how you will display it. The most obvious way to display your quilt is to have it framed professionally. Another way you can display the quilt is to stretch it over a blank canvas. If you want to stretch it on a canvas you will not need to add a backing, batting or a binding. Center it over the canvas, then use a staple gun

to secure the quilt top to the wooden frame of the canvas. Another way that I like to display my quilts is to add a sleeve to the back of the quilt as shown in the diagram below. To add a sleeve, just make a 4" fabric tube the width of the quilt, then hand stitch it to the top of the quilt on both sides of the tube. To hang the quilt you will need a cafe curtain rod. Apply the curtain rod hardware to the wall according to the manufacturer's instructions. Pull the curtain rod through the sleeve to hang the quilt. You can buy cafe curtain rods at any hardware store.

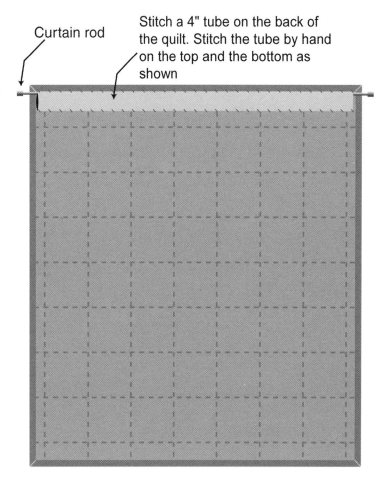

Curtain rod

Stitch a 4" tube on the back of the quilt. Stitch the tube by hand on the top and the bottom as shown

"Instead of trying to reproduce exactly what I have before my eyes, I use color more arbitrarily, in order to express myself more forcibly."

Vincent Van Gogh, August 1888

Chapter 6

Quilted Photo Patterns

In this chapter

Explaining The Patterns

You will notice that the Color Palette is always arranged in order, with #1 being the lightest color and #24 being the darkest. The palettes in this chapter that are shown in color are suggested colors based on the colors in the original photograph. If you choose your fabrics based on the shown color palette, your quilt will have a realistic appearance. The palettes that are shown in black, white and gray are just a representation of color values and you will choose your own colors.

The numbers inside the color boxes are estimates of the numbers of fabric squares you will need of each color. You will use these numbers to determine how much yardage you will need of each of the 24 fabrics (See the yardage chart later in this chapter).

The next thing you must pay attention to is the Palette Suggestions list. The palette suggestions are a list of all the possible color palettes that were explained in chapter 2. Within each Palette Suggestion list I have only included the types of palettes that are suitable for that pattern.

The last and most important part of the pattern is the Pattern Grid. Each Pattern Grid contains numbered squares that correspond with your sorted and numbered fabrics. The larger grid sections represent the grid guide. When you follow the Pattern Grid while placing the fabric squares, you will recreate the photograph shown.

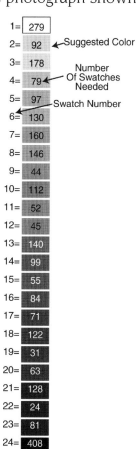

How To Use The Grid Guide

The grid guide is a printed grid that is made up of squares that are the same size as the fabric squares you will use for your quilt. The grid guide that is included with this book has 1¼" on one side and 1½" on the other side. To use the grid guide, place it under the fusible interfacing (adhesive side facing up) as a guide for arranging the fabric swatches.

Transfer the numbers from the Pattern Grid to the Grid Guide, one section at a time.

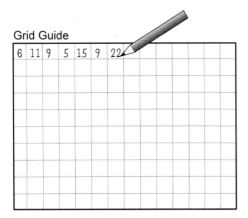

Grid Guide

Use a soft pencil to write the numbers into the grid (3B soft pencil). The soft lead is dark enough to see through the interfacing and it is easy to erase.

After you apply the first section of fabric squares and iron them in place, erase the numbers and transfer the second section of numbers to the grid guide. Line up the grid guide the same way that it appears in the Pattern Grid and repeat the process.

If the pattern has a straight grid then put the guide under the interfacing the same way it appears. If the pattern is on an angle then use the following instructions for positioning the grid guide.

You will need a quilting ruler that has a 30 degree or a 60 degree mark on it. Line up the 30 or 60 degree angle with the straight edge of the interfacing as shown in the diagram A on page 39.

Mark a 30 degree line as shown in the diagram. Next you will line up the edge of the grid with the angled line you have drawn(diagram B, on page 39). Continue placing the squares according to the angled Pattern Grid.

I have prepared more Quilted Photography patterns for you on my website. To get them, come visit me at www.QuiltedPhoto.com. To get the additional patterns you will need the access code located in the lower right corner of page 77.

Place grid guide on the table

8	4	2	4	9	5	3	9	3	2	11	4	3	4
5	8	4	2	4	9	5	3	9	3	2	11	4	3
4	2	4	9	5	3	9	3	2	11	4	3	1	1
8	4	2	4	9	5	3	9	3	2	11	4	3	4
5	8	4	2	4	9	5	3	9	3	2	11	4	3
4	2	4	9	5	3	9	3	2	11	4	3	1	1
8	4	2	4	9	5	3	9	3	2	11	4	3	4
5	8	4	2	4	9	5	3	9	3	2	11	4	3
4	2	4	9	5	3	9	3	2	11	4	3	1	1
8	4	2	4	9	5	3	9	3	2	11	4	3	4

Place fusible interfacing on top of the grid guide

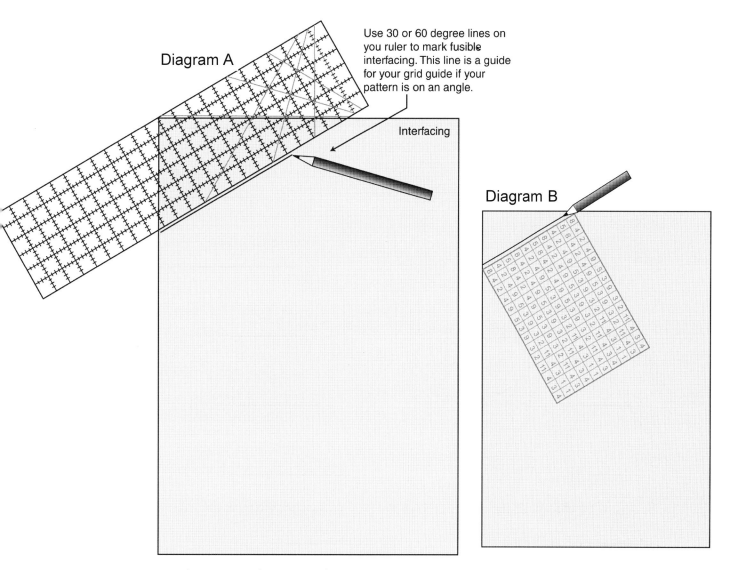

Diagram A

Use 30 or 60 degree lines on you ruler to mark fusible interfacing. This line is a guide for your grid guide if your pattern is on an angle.

Interfacing

Diagram B

How To Determine Fabric Requirements

The colored numbers in the pattern palette, are used along with the size of the square to figure the yardage requirement. The yardage requirements are based on 44"/45" wide fabrics.

	1/16th yard	1/8th yard	¼ yard	½ yard
1" squares	94	188	376	752
1 ¼" squares	55	110	220	440
1 ½" squares	46	92	184	368
2" squares	23	46	92	184

Rosebud Pattern

1	131
2	70
3	72
4	73
5	58
6	105
7	64
8	46
9	39
10	56
11	73
12	58
13	46
14	45
15	41
16	35
17	42
18	32
19	33
20	22
21	23
22	25
23	32
24	89

Suggested Color Palettes

☐ Random Color
☒ Single Color
☐ Restricted Color
☐ Realistic Color

Approximate Finished Sizes

	Width	Length
1¼"	26"	22"
1½"	35"	30"

Interfacing Needed = 2 yards

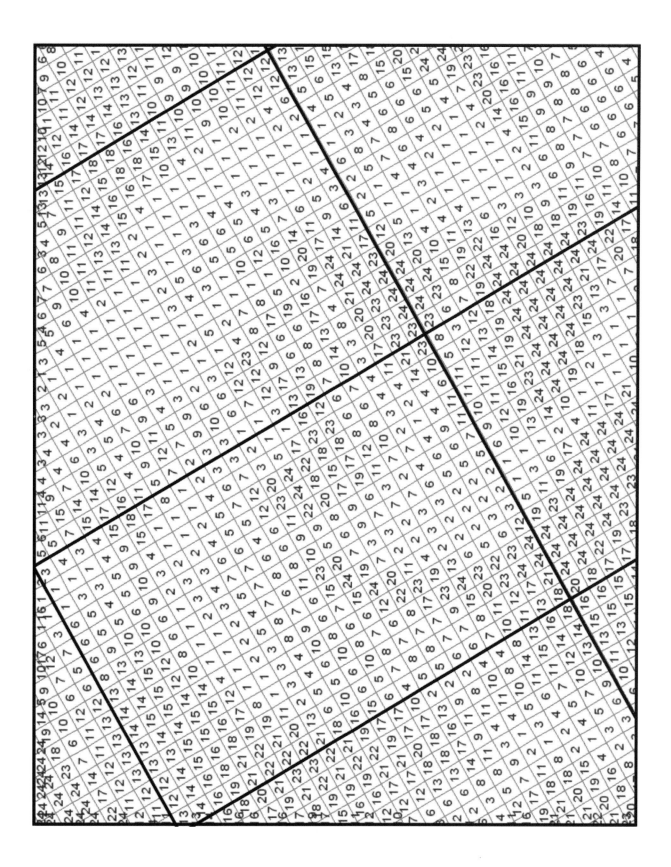

Money Pattern

1	807
2	146
3	46
4	107
5	4
6	60
7	71
8	84
9	101
10	92
11	91
12	112
13	100
14	125
15	136
16	140
17	100
18	147
19	79
20	72
21	59
22	73
23	68
24	204

2	19	22	19	19	16	13	18	15	21	18	15	20	16	17	23	22	22	23	23	23	24	20	18	19	18	15	19	17	16	15	14	15	14	16	10	14	14
2	19	17	20	14	13	13	13	12	18	18	18	15	18	19	18	18	18	18	19	18	18	18	17	16	14	13	15	14	15	13	12	11	9	7	4	9	9
2	18	14	18	4	2	1	1	7	18	18	18	18	19	15	19	17	17	17	17	17	18	14	13	17	14	12	8	6	8	10	11	13	15	17	10	20	14
2	14	15	17	9	7	4	7	17	13	13	13	16	8	15	8	7	3	3	4	4	4	10	10	9	9	10	14	16	16	16	13	14	17	19	11	13	16
2	12	16	14	17	21	19	22	20	11	20	19	8	2	11	16	12	15	15	11	13	14	14	13	10	19	12	18	14	15	16	14	14	14	12	8	9	9
1	15	19	20	16	15	7	2	14	20	21	16	8	2	2	18	10	19	18	14	16	12	13	14	12	13	13	15	12	11	9	9	4	1	1	1	1	1
2	15	17	18	11	14	16	1	2	21	17	10	4	1	1	13	12	14	15	13	13	14	9	10	9	9	6	3	1	1	1	1	1	1	1	1	1	4
2	16	15	13	1	2	16	1	1	16	9	2	1	1	1	1	2	9	10	9	9	7	9	7	10	9	7	9	9	8	1	1	1	1	1	1	6	20
2	17	16	14	4	7	15	1	2	18	7	1	1	1	1	7	10	9	7	10	10	10	9	11	10	8	11	8	11	10	10	3	1	1	1	2	20	24
2	19	23	19	12	14	9	4	17	15	1	1	1	1	1	2	4	3	4	4	6	4	3	6	4	2	4	2	2	3	2	2	1	1	2	15	24	24
2	18	22	20	16	19	18	20	14	1	1	1	1	1	1	1	1	1	1	1	1	1	1	1	1	1	1	1	1	1	1	1	1	1	7	23	24	21
2	18	13	18	14	12	11	2	1	1	1	1	1	1	1	1	1	1	1	1	1	1	1	1	1	1	1	1	1	1	1	1	1	2	15	24	24	23
2	19	21	22	15	13	4	11	4	1	1	2	10	1	1	1	1	1	1	1	3	3	1	1	1	1	1	1	1	1	1	1	1	2	22	24	24	20
2	18	24	23	15	9	1	4	2	1	1	11	12	1	1	1	11	18	18	17	16	4	1	1	1	1	1	1	1	1	1	1	1	9	24	24	22	15
2	19	23	23	15	11	1	1	1	1	1	8	12	2	1	1	1	12	18	19	18	19	16	17	6	1	1	1	1	1	1	1	1	13	24	24	21	19
2	15	21	20	15	10	1	1	1	1	1	1	1	1	1	1	4	17	19	12	9	10	15	19	14	1	1	1	1	1	1	1	1	15	24	23	22	20
2	15	16	17	14	10	1	1	1	1	1	1	1	1	1	1	10	19	15	3	18	12	6	21	15	1	1	1	1	1	1	1	1	16	24	23	23	21
2	17	18	19	15	10	1	1	1	1	1	1	1	1	1	1	10	18	12	1	20	10	1	19	19	3	1	1	1	1	1	1	1	16	24	23	22	22
2	15	18	18	13	9	1	1	1	1	1	1	1	1	1	1	9	21	19	6	18	3	8	23	18	1	1	1	1	1	1	1	2	16	24	24	22	23
2	15	19	18	15	9	2	1	1	1	1	1	1	1	1	1	2	18	18	16	12	13	19	18	11	1	1	1	1	1	1	1	7	14	24	24	21	22
2	18	22	22	14	16	14	1	1	1	1	1	1	1	1	1	1	5	19	19	17	18	20	14	1	1	1	1	1	1	1	1	12	12	24	24	23	22
2	19	24	23	16	17	2	1	1	1	1	1	1	1	1	1	1	1	4	13	15	15	10	1	1	1	1	1	1	1	1	1	11	11	22	24	24	23
1	17	22	22	16	16	2	1	1	1	1	1	1	1	1	1	1	1	1	1	1	1	1	1	1	1	1	1	1	1	1	1	10	17	15	24	24	24
2	19	22	18	17	15	12	1	1	1	1	1	1	1	1	1	1	1	1	1	1	3	2	1	1	2	2	1	1	1	1	1	1	13	12	23	24	24
2	18	16	18	14	16	16	8	1	1	1	7	7	1	1	1	3	8	4	2	4	4	1	3	3	2	1	1	4	1	1	1	1	10	14	15	24	24
2	14	16	1	1	1	18	14	1	1	1	14	10	1	1	1	2	4	8	9	7	4	10	9	9	4	9	9	10	8	7	1	1	9	16	18	16	24
2	16	13	16	18	20	18	14	1	1	1	11	10	1	1	1	1	4	7	4	4	7	7	9	9	9	6	2	4	1	1	1	1	1	10	16	11	17
2	17	14	16	8	8	15	14	1	1	1	1	1	1	1	1	1	1	1	4	11	12	12	12	12	12	12	11	11	11	11	11	11	11	13	15	15	14
2	16	11	6	13	1	16	15	6	2	1	1	1	1	1	1	1	1	1	6	15	20	18	17	18	17	17	17	17	17	18	17	17	18	16	19	18	18
2	14	10	7	12	1	17	17	17	17	16	13	8	4	1	1	1	1	9	4	12	19	14	1	14	16	8	14	12	2	17	19	2	14	15	21	11	9
2	16	18	16	11	16	16	16	11	12	20	21	20	15	11	9	4	7	14	11	17	18	11	3	16	21	6	12	18	4	16	16	3	16	11	20	9	9
3	20	20	17	16	18	22	16	16	15	20	23	20	18	14	19	11	20	16	17	19	16	20	22	23	23	23	22	22	22	21	23	23	22	23	23	23

Suggested Color Palettes

☐ Random Color
☒ Single Color
☒ Restricted Color
☐ Realistic Color

Interfacing Needed = 3½ yards

Note: To make this quilt look like real money, you will need to choose only green fabrics from the lightest to the darkest shades. See chapter 2 for details about choosing color palettes.

Approximate Finished Sizes

	Width	Length
1¼"	63"	24"
1½"	84"	32"

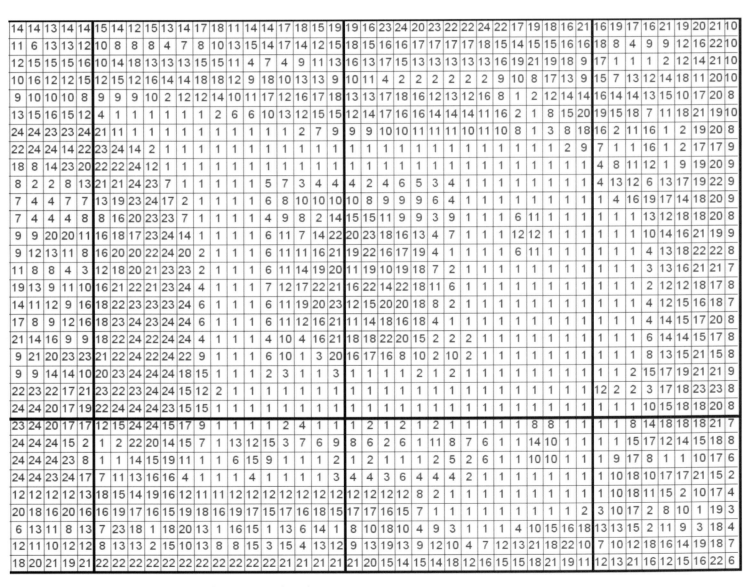

Note: This photograph and the pattern has been modified slightly as not to violate of the U.S. Code regarding the reproduction of currency (chapter 25 of Title 18).

Mona Lisa Pattern

1	58
2	116
3	74
4	53
5	58
6	41
7	30
8	10
9	11
10	25
11	34
12	16
13	18
14	23
15	24
16	21
17	24
18	29
19	31
20	25
21	26
22	42
23	93
24	322

Suggested Color Palettes

[x] Random Color
[x] Single Color
[x] Restricted Color
[ ] Realistic Color

Approximate Finished Sizes

	Width	Length
1¼"	19"	28"
1½"	25"	37"

Interfacing Needed = 2 yards

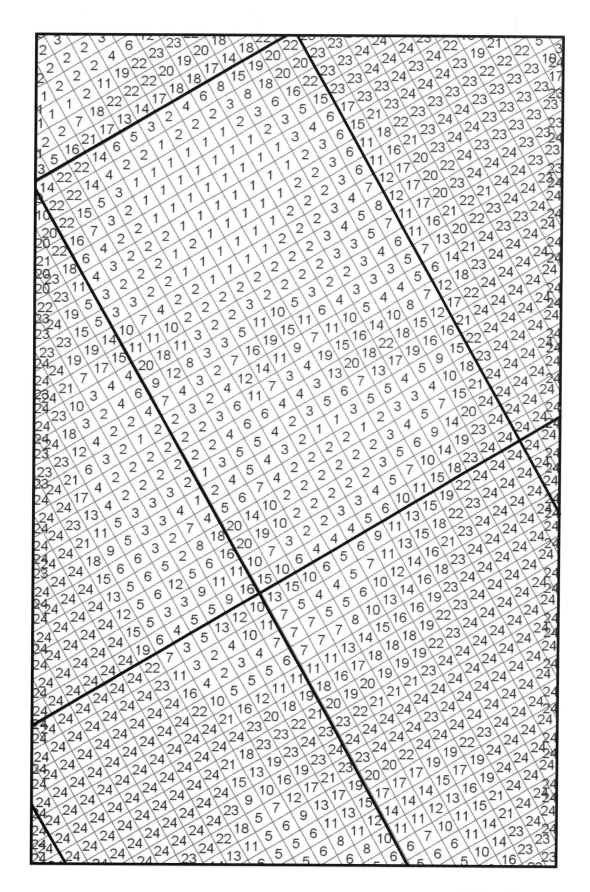

Lion Pattern

1	41
2	36
3	68
4	102
5	67
6	75
7	30
8	57
9	18
10	50
11	11
12	27
13	59
14	17
15	51
16	18
17	53
18	52
19	49
20	8
21	21
22	43
23	36
24	151

Suggested Color Palettes

☐ Random Color
☒ Single Color
☒ Restricted Color
☐ Realistic Color

Approximate Finished Sizes

	Width	Length
1¼"	20"	25"
1½"	26"	34"

Interfacing Needed = 2 yards

23	23	19	19	17	21	22	19	18	19	19	19	19	21	23	24	22	21	19	19	17	13	13	17	17	17
18	18	22	19	19	23	19	17	17	21	19	19	17	18	22	22	22	21	17	18	18	15	15	15	17	15
19	17	18	8	18	22	19	19	17	18	19	15	13	13	18	19	19	19	19	19	19	18	17	15	15	13
23	22	17	10	18	23	19	17	17	19	17	12	10	10	13	15	15	16	13	13	17	19	18	17	15	13
21	19	12	16	21	21	18	17	17	17	13	10	6	6	6	8	15	13	6	6	8	15	18	17	15	13
24	24	22	22	21	21	15	15	15	17	15	8	6	4	4	6	10	12	6	4	5	11	17	13	15	15
24	24	23	18	17	13	8	10	15	19	13	8	7	6	4	6	12	12	6	3	3	5	16	13	13	8
24	24	22	18	15	13	13	10	16	18	12	6	4	3	3	6	12	11	7	3	2	2	7	10	13	10
24	23	18	19	13	10	12	13	15	12	8	6	4	4	2	2	5	7	5	2	2	1	4	6	10	13
22	19	13	11	8	6	8	13	10	7	7	7	4	4	6	1	2	5	5	5	2	1	4	5	10	13
22	12	7	8	6	4	8	10	8	7	6	5	4	3	10	2	2	3	7	6	3	2	6	5	7	12
18	6	4	15	6	4	8	10	6	5	4	6	6	3	6	3	4	3	6	8	3	3	4	4	6	10
8	4	8	17	8	6	8	6	5	7	5	11	12	9	6	5	4	3	4	6	3	5	7	18	18	10
6	6	17	15	8	8	8	5	5	9	18	22	12	22	16	4	5	4	3	6	3	6	11	18	9	8
5	12	19	13	8	8	8	4	4	3	4	14	19	23	22	3	7	4	3	5	4	6	14	9	4	8
6	13	17	13	10	10	8	5	3	4	7	9	3	3	14	14	5	4	3	5	6	5	7	5	7	8
6	8	17	17	13	10	8	4	4	4	4	11	9	5	7	9	8	4	3	3	8	5	8	7	8	10
6	6	15	15	13	13	10	6	6	4	5	6	7	7	9	9	7	4	3	3	4	3	4	11	10	10
6	6	13	15	13	13	10	6	4	4	4	5	7	9	9	7	5	3	3	4	3	4	4	6	12	10
6	6	13	15	10	15	10	6	4	4	5	4	4	6	5	5	5	2	3	4	3	3	3	3	12	13
6	6	10	18	13	15	10	6	4	4	4	4	3	4	5	7	4	4	4	5	4	4	4	3	8	15
6	6	8	17	15	15	15	10	6	4	3	2	3	2	4	5	4	5	6	5	4	4	4	3	5	16
4	8	8	15	15	15	17	15	8	4	2	2	3	3	3	3	6	6	7	5	5	4	4	4	4	16
6	12	8	15	15	15	18	13	10	6	4	3	2	4	3	4	5	6	5	5	5	4	3	4	3	11
6	12	8	17	15	17	19	17	13	5	4	4	2	4	4	4	4	9	3	3	4	4	4	3	3	7
8	7	8	18	15	17	22	19	18	12	4	4	3	4	4	5	3	14	22	14	18	14	9	11	14	11
12	16	10	17	15	17	22	22	22	18	5	2	2	3	3	4	4	2	14	24	24	24	23	22	14	5
13	21	12	17	15	17	21	24	22	12	5	2	2	2	1	3	3	3	1	5	14	24	24	11	1	5
14	22	18	18	16	17	21	24	23	16	9	2	3	1	2	3	3	3	1	1	1	20	11	1	1	9
16	22	23	19	19	18	23	24	24	24	22	11	14	5	2	2	2	1	1	1	1	14	1	1	5	22
19	22	23	24	23	21	24	24	24	24	23	20	20	18	5	3	2	1	1	1	11	22	3	2	18	22
22	23	23	24	24	23	24	24	24	24	24	24	24	22	18	11	3	2	3	14	14	9	3	14	24	24
23	22	24	24	23	24	24	24	24	24	24	24	24	24	7	5	5	5	3	7	4	1	1	9	24	24
24	24	24	24	23	24	24	24	24	24	24	24	24	24	14	1	1	1	1	1	1	1	1	9	24	24

Statue Pattern

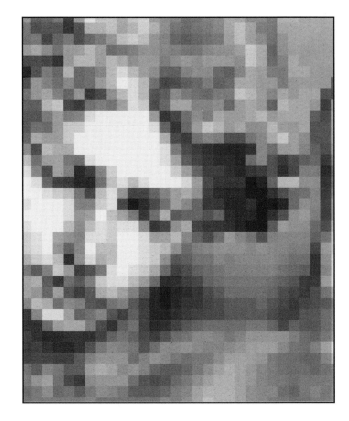

1	66
2	42
3	34
4	39
5	73
6	59
7	61
8	71
9	76
10	67
11	88
12	75
13	72
14	45
15	34
16	29
17	28
18	27
19	23
20	27
21	12
22	8
23	17
24	7

Suggested Color Palettes

[x] Random Color
[x] Single Color
[x] Restricted Color
[ ] Realistic Color

Approximate Finished Sizes

	Width	Length
1¼"	22"	25"
1½"	30"	34"

Interfacing Needed = 2 yards

12	17	15	15	21	16	5	5	4	7	5	3	5	9	12	13	12	11	10	6	4	7	11	12	6	6	6	6	6
12	11	17	13	11	16	13	11	8	4	3	4	8	10	13	14	13	12	11	6	4	7	9	13	8	6	6	7	7
7	5	8	11	7	6	4	6	13	11	9	7	8	9	11	11	11	9	8	8	6	3	6	13	8	6	6	7	7	6
16	15	16	18	7	4	4	5	4	5	8	7	7	10	8	7	8	7	6	7	8	3	5	12	9	5	7	6	6	6
23	14	9	13	4	12	11	9	4	2	4	6	8	13	13	9	8	8	12	13	9	5	6	10	10	5	5	6	6	7
15	7	9	11	8	12	11	6	4	1	2	4	11	16	15	13	12	10	13	12	5	5	7	8	10	7	5	5	7	14
11	7	5	10	11	6	17	14	7	3	2	4	13	13	8	10	11	11	10	10	3	5	6	9	5	8	5	5	14	15
13	13	4	4	16	18	11	10	11	7	2	3	16	11	5	5	9	9	8	12	5	5	7	13	4	5	5	7	17	7
14	14	10	6	11	9	3	1	1	1	1	1	7	19	15	10	8	10	5	6	7	5	4	6	5	5	5	12	15	5
14	11	12	7	3	3	1	1	1	1	1	1	2	13	19	13	6	3	4	7	5	8	7	5	6	7	5	13	14	5
13	5	8	6	3	1	1	1	1	1	1	1	1	5	16	17	11	9	10	15	15	11	9	5	3	6	8	14	14	5
10	16	3	5	5	1	1	1	1	1	1	1	1	2	11	17	18	20	22	23	23	20	9	12	6	6	9	13	15	7
4	12	6	5	12	11	2	1	1	1	1	1	1	2	6	14	17	19	21	21	23	13	9	15	17	15	13	12	18	9
2	10	16	5	10	22	18	9	3	1	1	1	1	1	3	7	13	18	18	20	22	19	18	16	20	16	10	10	21	12
1	3	13	18	19	21	22	13	4	2	3	2	1	1	1	2	7	16	19	19	19	23	23	13	5	5	8	8	20	11
1	1	2	3	5	11	17	4	2	8	17	16	13	9	6	5	8	18	21	20	22	23	24	20	14	12	11	8	18	9
2	1	1	1	2	10	10	3	2	17	23	21	16	12	7	9	13	19	19	23	22	20	24	24	20	12	8	9	17	6
2	1	1	1	2	8	7	1	4	7	12	19	12	5	14	13	13	15	13	20	23	21	24	20	15	8	7	10	17	6
2	1	1	1	4	9	4	2	3	2	2	9	19	17	8	5	17	19	19	20	22	24	24	13	7	8	8	11	15	4
3	2	1	6	8	10	2	2	3	1	1	2	7	6	4	9	13	16	12	7	9	11	15	9	9	9	9	13	12	3
3	2	1	9	13	9	1	3	4	1	1	1	3	4	8	12	10	9	8	8	8	9	8	9	9	9	9	15	8	3
5	3	2	5	20	8	2	5	4	1	1	2	3	8	14	13	11	10	9	9	9	9	9	9	10	11	11	19	8	2
11	14	11	3	7	18	16	11	2	1	2	3	5	13	17	15	13	12	11	10	10	10	10	10	11	12	13	19	10	2
6	5	14	19	11	14	10	3	2	2	4	7	12	20	20	17	16	13	12	11	11	11	11	12	13	14	18	18	7	2
7	8	13	7	15	18	14	5	4	6	10	14	20	24	23	21	19	16	14	12	12	12	12	13	15	16	18	15	11	5
9	4	5	12	9	9	13	15	11	11	14	18	23	23	21	19	19	17	16	14	14	14	13	15	16	18	16	15	14	10
19	8	2	2	6	13	11	9	14	17	13	17	23	23	20	18	17	16	16	14	14	14	14	16	17	17	15	14	12	9
20	20	12	6	5	5	10	15	19	13	12	17	21	20	17	14	13	13	12	12	12	11	11	13	16	13	14	14	12	8
18	20	23	21	20	20	20	18	13	11	13	16	18	15	12	10	9	9	10	11	10	8	8	8	8	10	12	13	11	7
18	18	20	22	23	20	15	11	9	10	11	15	12	9	9	8	9	10	10	9	8	7	6	7	9	11	12	10	7	2
18	17	17	18	18	15	10	8	8	8	12	10	8	9	11	12	11	11	9	7	6	7	8	11	12	12	13	13	10	4
12	14	10	12	14	14	8	5	6	9	9	10	13	14	14	13	11	9	7	5	6	6	8	9	11	12	12	13	12	10
11	8	6	12	17	19	9	8	8	8	12	15	16	15	13	11	9	7	5	5	6	8	10	11	12	12	11	11	11	10
13	11	9	13	12	14	10	9	10	11	14	14	14	13	11	10	7	5	5	5	7	9	10	10	12	13	11	10	11	9

Fruit Pattern

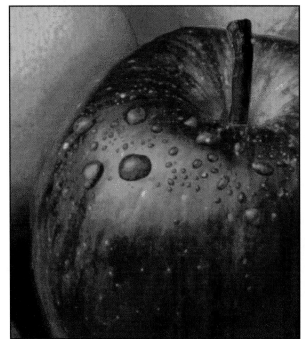
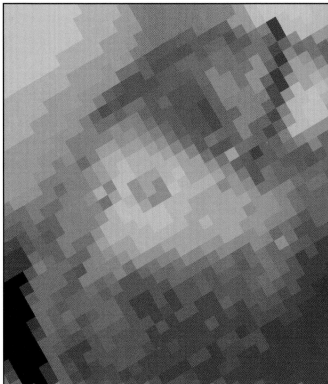

1	13
2	17
3	50
4	22
5	45
6	44
7	60
8	45
9	30
10	44
11	59
12	21
13	30
14	28
15	81
16	89
17	33
18	72
19	91
20	44
21	41
22	68
23	56
24	29

Suggested Color Palettes

☐ Random Color
☐ Single Color
☐ Restricted Color
☒ Realistic Color

Approximate Finished Sizes

	Width	Length
1¼"	34"	37"
1½"	45"	49"

Interfacing Needed = 2¼ yards

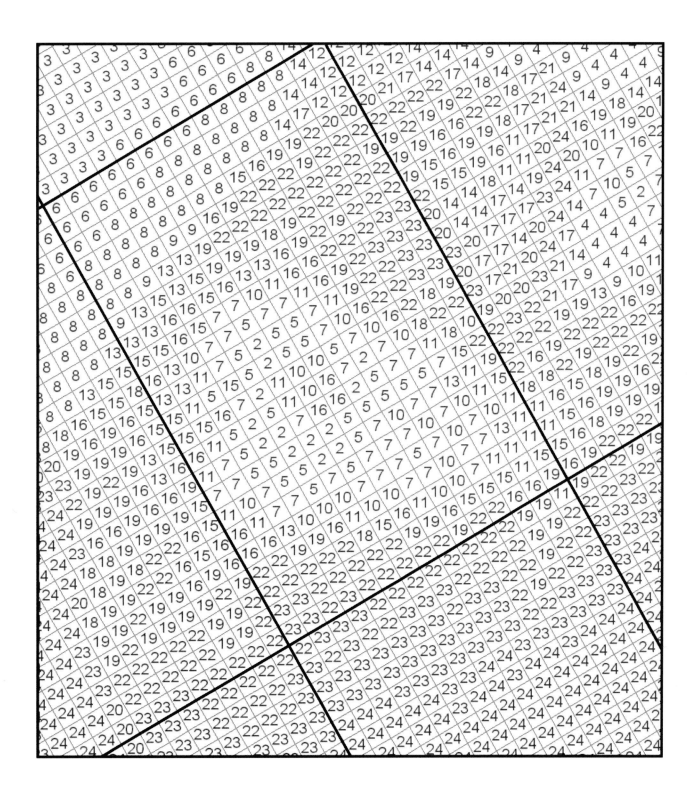

USA Flag Pattern

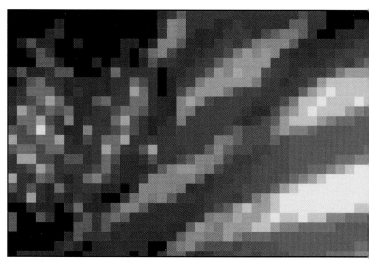

1	44
2	43
3	19
4	46
5	41
6	20
7	28
8	40
9	29
10	27
11	34
12	19
13	65
14	33
15	24
16	50
17	28
18	21
19	53
20	61
21	67
22	44
23	80
24	124

Suggested Color Palettes

☐ Random Color
☐ Single Color
☐ Restricted Color
☒ Realistic Color

Approximate Finished Sizes

	Width	Length
1¼"	30"	19"
1½"	40"	26"

Interfacing Needed = 1 yards

Note: To make this quilt look like an American Flag, you will need to choose your fabrics according to the suggested color palette. See chapter 2 for details about choosing color palettes.

Kitty Pattern

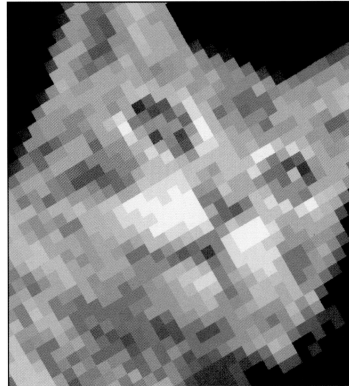

1	32
2	39
3	28
4	30
5	34
6	56
7	37
8	59
9	71
10	58
11	33
12	44
13	72
14	58
15	53
16	42
17	46
18	10
19	20
20	25
21	19
22	15
23	27
24	206

Suggested Color Palettes

☐ Random Color
☐ Single Color
☒ Restricted Color
☒ Realistic Color

Approximate Finished Sizes

	Width	Length
1¼"	34"	37"
1½"	45"	49"

Interfacing Needed = 2¼ yards

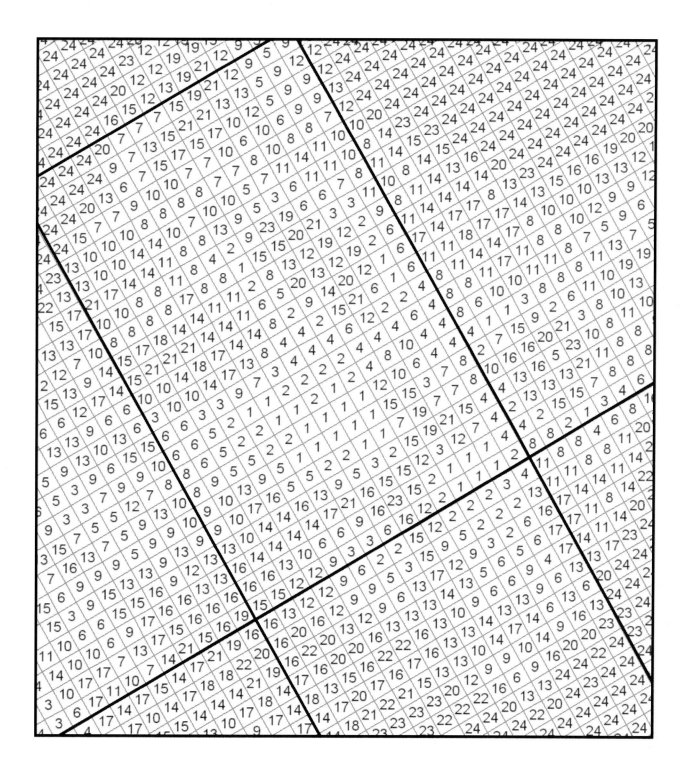

Sunset Pattern

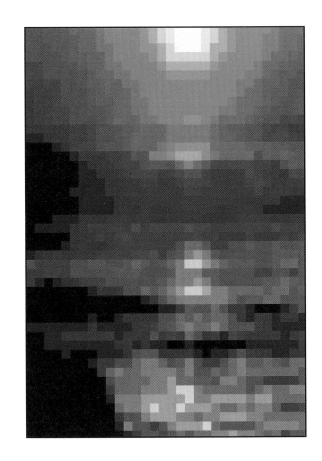

1	9
2	5
3	20
4	18
5	33
6	24
7	92
8	46
9	50
10	22
11	63
12	11
13	85
14	38
15	43
16	48
17	110
18	62
19	50
20	100
21	130
22	103
23	103
24	207

Suggested Color Palettes

☐ Random Color
☐ Single Color
☐ Restricted Color
☒ Realistic Color

Approximate Finished Sizes

	Width	Length
1¼"	22"	34"
1½"	30"	46"

Interfacing Needed = 2 yards

18	18	15	15	14	12	11	11	8	7	7	7	7	6	4	3	2	1	1	1	2	3	4	6	7	7	7	7	8	11
18	18	15	15	14	14	11	11	8	7	7	7	7	6	4	3	2	1	1	1	2	3	4	6	7	7	7	8	8	11
18	18	18	15	15	14	11	11	8	8	7	7	7	6	6	4	3	1	1	1	2	4	4	6	7	7	7	8	8	11
18	18	18	18	15	14	14	11	11	8	7	7	7	7	6	4	3	3	3	3	3	4	6	7	7	7	7	8	11	11
19	19	18	18	18	15	14	11	11	8	8	7	7	7	7	6	4	4	4	4	4	6	7	7	7	7	8	11	11	14
19	19	18	18	18	18	15	14	11	11	8	8	7	7	7	7	6	6	6	6	6	7	7	7	7	8	8	11	14	15
20	20	19	19	18	18	15	14	14	11	11	8	8	7	7	7	7	7	7	7	7	7	7	8	8	11	14	14	15	
21	20	20	19	18	18	18	15	14	11	11	11	8	7	7	7	7	7	7	7	7	7	7	8	11	11	14	15	15	
21	20	20	19	18	18	18	15	14	14	11	11	8	8	7	7	7	7	7	7	7	7	8	11	11	11	14	15	18	
21	20	20	19	19	18	18	15	15	14	11	11	8	8	7	7	7	7	7	7	7	8	8	11	11	14	15	18	18	
21	20	20	19	19	18	18	18	15	14	12	11	11	8	8	7	7	7	6	6	7	8	11	11	12	14	15	18	18	19
22	22	21	21	21	20	20	19	18	18	15	14	14	12	11	11	8	8	8	8	8	11	14	15	15	18	18	19	20	20
23	23	22	21	21	20	20	19	18	18	15	14	11	11	11	11	8	8	8	8	8	11	14	14	15	18	18	19	19	19
24	24	24	23	22	20	19	19	18	15	15	14	11	11	11	8	7	6	6	6	6	11	11	11	11	14	14	14	15	15
24	24	24	24	24	23	21	21	21	20	20	19	15	15	7	7	6	4	4	4	6	8	11	11	11	12	17	14	15	14
24	24	24	24	24	24	23	22	21	21	20	19	19	18	15	15	18	12	7	11	15	19	19	19	19	19	20	20	21	17
24	24	24	24	24	24	23	23	22	22	21	20	19	19	19	20	20	19	18	18	20	21	21	21	21	19	20	21	21	22
24	24	24	24	24	24	23	23	23	22	22	21	21	20	20	21	21	20	19	19	20	21	21	21	21	20	19	20	21	21
24	24	24	24	24	23	23	23	23	22	22	21	21	21	21	21	21	21	21	21	21	21	21	21	22	22	22	22	22	23
24	24	24	24	24	24	23	23	23	23	22	22	22	21	22	22	21	21	21	21	21	22	22	22	22	22	22	23	23	23
24	24	24	23	23	23	22	22	22	22	21	21	21	21	21	22	21	21	21	21	22	22	22	22	21	21	21	21	22	22
24	23	23	23	23	22	21	20	20	20	20	20	17	20	19	19	19	19	17	19	19	20	20	20	20	20	20	20	19	20
24	24	24	24	24	22	22	21	20	21	20	19	20	20	20	20	20	20	20	19	20	20	21	21	21	20	21	21	21	20
24	24	24	24	23	22	21	22	22	21	20	20	20	20	20	20	20	17	12	12	16	20	20	17	17	16	17	17	16	17
23	22	22	21	22	21	21	21	20	20	20	20	19	19	17	20	17	16	10	5	10	16	17	17	17	17	17	17	16	16
17	20	20	20	20	17	17	16	16	17	17	16	13	16	17	16	13	10	3	3	5	10	13	16	16	16	17	17	16	13
21	21	20	20	20	17	17	17	17	17	16	16	16	17	17	17	16	10	10	10	16	16	17	17	17	17	20	20	17	17
22	23	24	23	22	22	20	20	20	17	17	17	17	17	17	16	13	10	10	5	10	16	17	17	17	17	17	16	16	13
24	24	24	24	24	24	23	22	22	21	17	17	13	16		13	9	5	3	3	4	10	9	13	13	13	13	16	13	13
24	24	24	24	24	24	24	24	24	24	24	24	24	23	22	17	13	10	10	10	10	10	10	13	17	16	16	13	13	17
24	24	24	24	24	24	24	24	24	24	24	24	24	24	24	23	23	21	16	17	17	13	17	22	22	23	24	24	24	23
24	24	24	24	24	24	23	24	24	23	22	22	22	22		17	17	13	16	12	16	13	13	17	22	23	22	22	23	22
23	23	23	23	23	23	23	22	23	23	23	23	22	21	20	17	16	12	9	13	13	9	13	17	17	17	21	22	23	23
24	24	23	23	22	22	22	22	22	21	23	22	22	22	17	21	20	21	13	17	22	21	23	20	21	22	22	22	22	23
24	24	23	23	23	23	23	23	23	23	22	22	23	23	23	23	24	24	23	24	24	24	24	24	24	23	23	23	23	23
24	24	24	24	23	24	24	23	23	23	22	17	16	16		22	22	22	22	23	24	23	23	21	17	21	22	22	23	23
24	24	24	24	24	24	24	23	21	21	17	17	13	9	9	13	17	16	9	17	21	21	17	13	9	16	16	13	16	17
24	24	24	24	24	24	24	24	21	13	9	13	13	9	9	9	9	13	10	17	17	13	16	13	9	13	13	13	13	13
24	24	24	24	24	24	24	24	17	13	13	13	13	9		9	5	13	13	16	16	17	9	9	13	17	17	21	22	22
24	24	24	24	24	24	24	24	24	21	13	13	13	9	9	10	5	3	3	9	13	13	13	13	13	17	13	9	13	13
24	24	24	24	24	24	24	24	24	23	9	9	9	5	5	5	5	5	3	10	9	5	5	5	5	9	5	5	13	13
24	24	24	24	24	24	24	24	24	24	13	9	9	5	3	5	5	3	5	5	5	9	13	13	9	13	9	9	16	21
24	24	24	24	24	24	24	24	24	22	17	17	9	5		5	5	10	9	13	9	9	5	5	5	9	9	13	13	13
24	24	24	24	24	24	24	24	24	24	23	9	17	17	21	17	10	5	5	5	5	3	13	17	17	17	17	13	9	9	9

Cherubs Pattern

Color Key

#	Value
1	279
2	92
3	178
4	79
5	97
6	130
7	160
8	146
9	44
10	112
11	52
12	45
13	140
14	99
15	55
16	84
17	71
18	122
19	31
20	63
21	128
22	24
23	81
24	408

Pattern Grid

1	1	1	1	1	1	1	1	1	1	1	1	1	1	1	1	1	2	5	9	14	14	17	20	21	21	21	21	19	5	1	1	1	1
1	1	1	1	1	1	1	1	1	1	1	1	1	1	1	1	5	13	14	17	20	21	21	21	24	24	24	24	21	17	5	2	1	1
1	1	1	1	1	1	1	1	1	1	1	1	1	1	2	2	13	17	20	14	20	21	21	24	24	24	23	21	23	21	16	5	1	1
1	1	1	1	1	1	1	1	1	1	1	1	1	1	1	2	14	20	17	17	17	20	21	24	21	23	20	21	23	24	21	17	5	1
1	1	1	1	1	1	1	1	1	1	1	1	1	1	1	9	20	20	17	17	17	20	21	24	17	17	20	21	24	24	21	14	5	2
1	1	1	1	1	1	1	1	1	1	1	1	1	1	2	3	21	20	20	17	14	17	17	21	7	14	21	23	21	21	24	21	13	2
1	1	1	1	1	1	1	1	1	1	1	1	1	1	4	7	23	20	20	17	14	14	17	14	5	7	17	21	21	18	24	21	13	5
1	1	1	1	1	1	1	1	1	1	1	1	1	1	2	6	21	23	21	20	14	14	14	7	5	7	10	14	18	21	21	21	14	5
2	8	11	19	19	22	19	19	19	19	11	8	2	2	2	7	20	23	23	20	17	17	14	7	7	14	14	13	17	13	18	16	13	2
22	24	24	24	24	24	22	22	22	22	22	19	17	13	5	4	21	24	21	20	21	20	17	10	16	21	17	7	10	14	10	13	2	1
11	24	24	24	24	24	24	24	24	24	24	21	20	17	20	7	20	23	21	21	21	17	17	13	7	5	10	5	5	10	10	13	11	3
1	11	24	24	24	24	24	24	24	24	24	24	24	23	23	24	21	20	17	20	21	20	14	10	7	5	5	5	14	17	13	13	11	4
1	11	19	24	24	24	24	24	24	24	24	24	24	24	24	24	24	21	17	20	21	17	10	7	5	5	5	5	5	10	14	14	11	3
1	1	11	24	24	24	24	24	24	24	24	24	24	24	24	24	24	21	21	21	14	7	5	5	5	7	7	10	13	7	7	14	13	5
2	1	2	19	24	24	24	24	23	23	23	23	24	24	24	24	21	16	13	9	14	17	10	7	5	5	7	7	10	13	7	10	20	18
2	1	2	11	19	21	23	23	23	23	23	23	23	23	23	3	5	5	5	5	5	13	14	10	10	7	10	10	10	10	14	13	21	18
2	2	2	2	2	9	18	23	23	23	23	23	23	20	9	5	5	5	5	5	5	7	9	10	13	13	14	13	13	10	10	16	23	21
2	2	2	2	2	2	18	23	23	23	23	23	23	9	5	5	5	5	5	5	7	7	7	9	13	16	13	7	5	9	14	21	21	19
2	2	2	2	2	11	16	20	20	23	23	23	13	5	5	5	5	5	5	7	9	9	7	9	13	16	9	7	13	18	21	24	21	18
2	2	2	2	2	2	11	16	18	20	20	13	7	5	5	5	5	5	7	10	10	7	7	7	13	16	7	5	13	20	24	21	16	16
2	3	3	4	2	3	2	4	16	16	13	7	7	5	5	5	7	10	13	13	9	7	7	7	10	14	5	5	7	14	18	13	13	14
4	4	4	4	4	4	4	4	4	9	7	7	7	7	7	10	10	14	16	13	9	7	7	10	13	14	7	5	7	7	13	13	14	16
4	4	4	4	4	4	4	6	9	7	7	7	7	7	7	10	13	20	17	10	7	7	10	13	16	9	5	5	5	5	9	14	16	17
6	6	6	6	6	6	6	11	9	7	7	7	7	7	7	13	18	21	16	10	7	7	10	9	13	17	9	5	5	5	7	13	18	20
8	6	6	6	6	6	6	9	7	7	7	7	10	10	13	16	21	24	16	13	9	9	10	13	16	18	10	5	5	5	7	10	16	18
12	12	8	12	8	6	8	7	5	7	9	13	13	16	20	8	16	23	20	16	13	13	14	16	18	21	10	7	5	7	7	10	14	18
12	12	12	12	12	12	11	7	5	9	14	14	13	9	13	13	14	14	14	14	13	14	18	21	24	13	7	7	7	7	7	10	14	18
15	12	15	15	12	12	13	7	7	7	5	5	7	7	7	7	7	7	7	7	7	7	10	13	17	24	16	7	7	7	7	10	16	21
15	15	15	15	12	15	13	7	7	7	7	7	7	7	7	7	7	7	7	7	7	7	10	10	17	21	13	7	7	7	10	13	20	21
22	19	22	19	19	19	16	14	13	10	10	10	7	7	10	10	10	10	10	10	7	7	7	10	7	14	23	20	13	13	13	16	21	24

Suggested Color Palettes

☐ Random Color
☐ Single Color
☐ Restricted Color
☒ Realistic Color

Approximate Finished Sizes

	Width	Length
1¼"	58"	22"
1½"	78"	30"

Interfacing Needed = 3½ yards

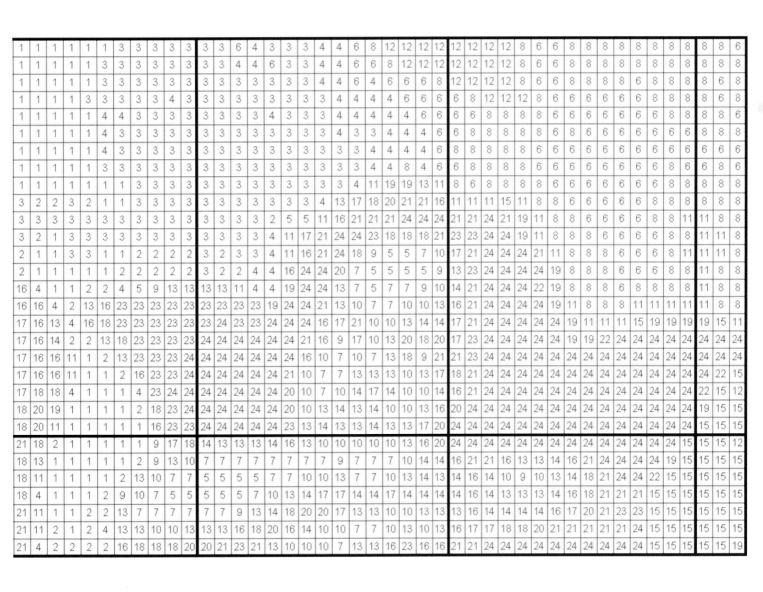

"Sheer work and calculation, with one's mind strained to the utmost, like an actor on the stage in a difficult part, with a thousand things to think of at once ...."

Vincent Van Gogh, July 1888

Gallery Of Quilts

In this chapter

The following pages are pictures of some of my Quilted Photos. These are quilts but also real photographs. I almost feel like I am inviting you into my home and showing you a personal photo album.

Some of the quilts are samples of the patterns in the previous chapter, but the rest of the quilts are portraits of my family, and friends.

Since the quilts are best viewed at a distance, you may have to hold the pages away from you to see the photographic images. As I have explained through out the book, you will only be able to see a beautiful collection of fabrics if you view the quilts close up. You can also see the photographic image easily if you look at the pictures in a mirror.

If you want to make Quilted Photos from your own photographs, go to www.QuiltedPhoto.com to learn how.

I am not sure that the photos of the quilts can conway the beauty of the quilts, but I hope you are inspired to make your own when you see my quilts.

Money Quilt

I love this money quilt! Everybody that sees it is intrigued by it. That includes men, children non-quilters and even teenagers! I think this quilt could be great to hang in an office, bank, or other commercial settings.

Cherubs Quilt

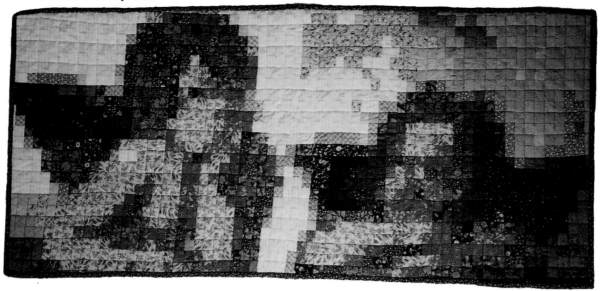

If you are a collector of angels you have to make this Quilted Photo. If you give it as a gift to someone who collects angels you will be loved forever! It has more fabric squares than some of the other patterns included in this book, but it is a work of art! You can find this pattern on page 58.

U.S. Flag Quilt

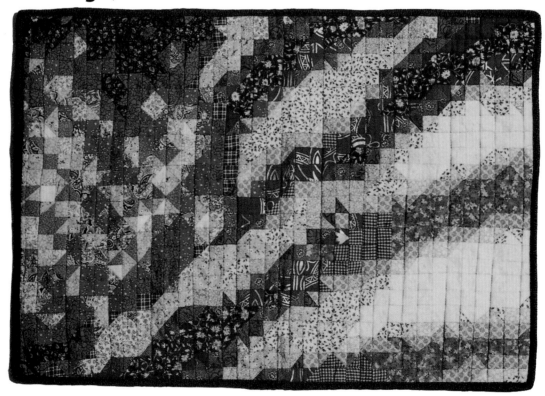

I experimented even further with this quilt by including half square triangles. It was a little more difficult to make then the quilts with all squares, but amazingly the stars sparkle! You can make a version of this quilt with just squares, and you will find the pattern on page 52. Come visit my website to get on my e-mail list so that you will be notified of new techniques such as these as they become available.

Mom n' Al Quilt

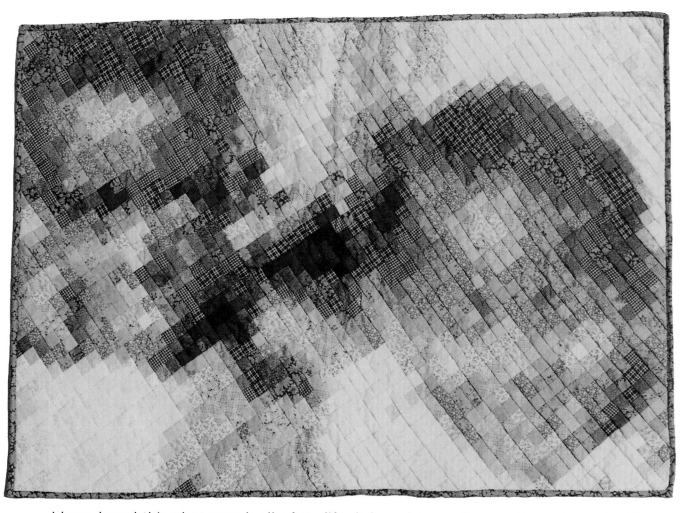

I have loved this photograph all of my life. It is a picture of my mother at age 4 with my uncle at age 7. It is amazing to me that in the quilt you can see my mom hugging my uncle's neck, and you can also see that he was not happy about it! This is an example of how a Quilted Photo can preserve a family memory.

Angela's Orange Quilt

This orange quilt is a picture of my daughter at one and a half years old. She is a happy child, and the quilt will always help me remember her at this stage of life.

Red Rose Quilt

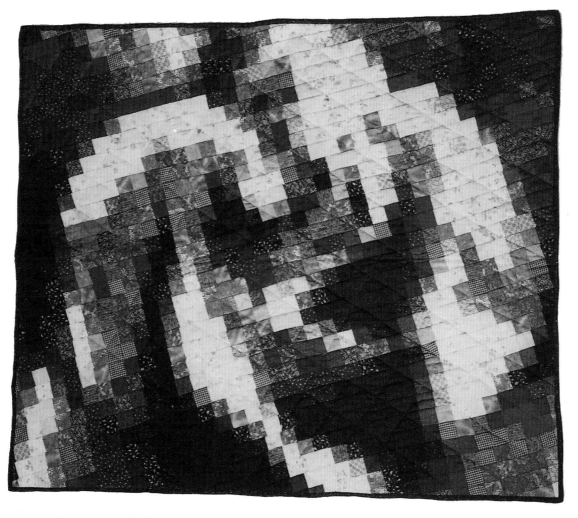

The rosebud quilt pattern is included in the previous chapter. It is more abstract than the rest of the patterns, but I think it is stunning, classic, and beautiful in this assortment of red fabrics.

Kitty Quilt

This kitty quilt is so gorgeous that I featured it on the cover of the book! This pattern is included in the book, but you can also make a quilted photo of your own pet!

Emily Quilt

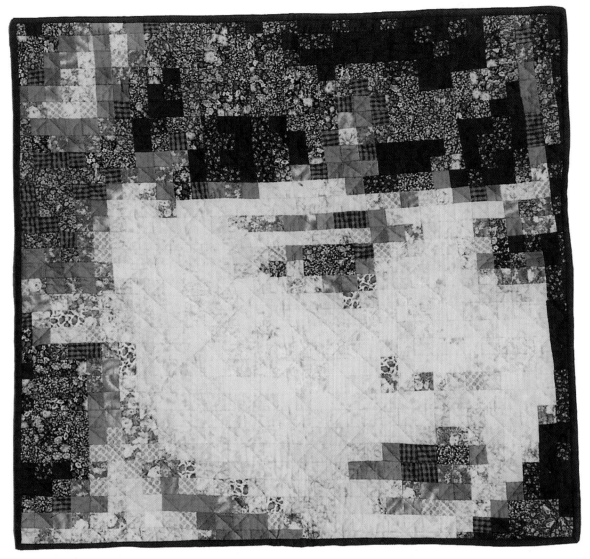

This quilted photo of Emily is one of my most beautiful quilted portraits! Her favorite colors are pink and purple, so her quilt is pink and purple. Emily's mother is an old friend of mine, and this quilt is a gift for her.

Bright Angie Quilt

I made this brightly colored quilt of my daughter Angela. While I was shopping for fabrics, I saw these fabrics and they reminded me of Angie's vibrant and energetic personality. This photo of her is at age two and a half. This is an example of how the fabric inspired me to make the quilt.

Lauren Quilt

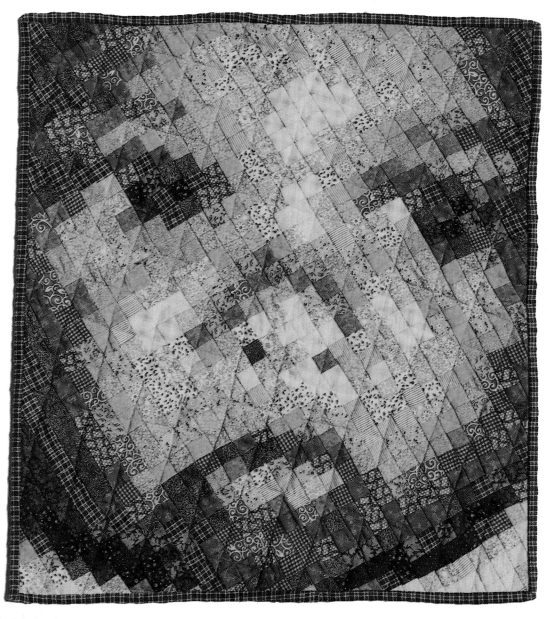

When I think about a baby quilt, this is what I think of! Since I have this quilt, I won't ever forget my niece's chubby cheeks, and poutey lips! This quilt really shows Lauren's personality. Make these close up baby quilts!...they are simply amazing gifts!

"The thing I hope to achieve
is to paint a good portrait."

Vincent Van Gogh, 1887

How To Make Your Own Quilted Photo Patterns

In this chapter

◆ Rules For Choosing A Photo To Quilt
◆ How Many Fabric Squares?
◆ Deciding What Color Palette To Use
◆ Should I Use A Straight Grid Or An Angled Grid?
◆ Making The Patterns

Rules for choosing a photo to quilt

The first rule that must be considered while choosing a photo is the light balance. It is ideal to have a balanced photograph that is not to light, or to dark. If the light areas of the image are really light, or if the dark areas are excessively dark, you will not be able to see the details of the image. If the image has a minor imbalance, it can be adjusted, but if the image is far out of balance, your quilt will not have clear details.

How Many Fabric Squares Should Your Quilted Photo Have?

The answer to this question depends on how much detail is in the image. If the image has a lot of small details then you will have to use more fabric squares to see the details clearly. If you decide to use to few squares, the image will look blurry. For a close-up image of a face, 1000 squares is enough to see the image clearly, but for a dollar bill or a building, the small details may dictate 3000 -4000 pieces. This is why I really enjoy using close-up views of faces, they have fewer pieces than the more detailed images, and they can be made in a very short period of time.

Balanced Photograph

Light Photograph

Dark Photograph

Photograph with lots of small details

1112 squares = Lost details

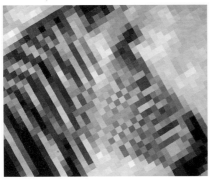

3424 squares = Clear details

Deciding What Color Palette To Use

There are several types of images that you can choose for quilting. I will explain each type of image and it's requirements.

Faces and hands happen to be my favorite images to quilt. They can be done with a color palette that is any combination of colors, realistic colors, or even a color combination that will match the colors of a room. The more outrageous the color, the more artistic people will think you are!

Animals or animal faces are fun to do also. Animals with fuzzy fur are best portrayed in color combinations that are realistic. If you use a random color palette for an animal, the image may be hard to see. If the animal has smooth fur, or skin any color combination that you choose will work fine. These are just my opinions, I urge you to be creative in your fabric and color choices because this is the most creative part of the whole quilted photo process.

Landscapes and Buildings have a lot of small details, so they need to have lots of dots to create the photo quilt. This also means that these quilts will be larger because they have many squares. Images of buildings can have any colors you choose, but the landscapes should have a realistic palette.

Other Objects like a bowl of fruit or flag or even a flower are best portrayed with realistic colors.

You can use old family pictures, or new snap shots, but you might want to consider using a digital camera to capture images for your quilts. The photographs will be created instantly and you can keep taking pictures until you get images you like.

A restricted or random color palette is good for faces, or hands. A single color palette is great for images that have only one color like a flower. A realistic color palette will work well with any image. Go to chapter 2 for more information about choosing a color palette.

Should You Use A Straight Grid Or An Angled Grid?

Your choice about what grid to use is just a matter of what you like most. The straight grid is slightly easier to sew, but the angled grid will give your quilt a more complicated look. The straight grid and the angled grid work equally well.

Making Your Patterns

To make your photographs into patterns you will need to scan your photo and save it as a file. You will then insert your photo file into computer software to translate it into a pattern for you. It is close to impossible to do it without the help of a computer, and you can get information about the available software at www.QuiltedPhoto.com

Straight Grid

Angled Grid

"The best pictures, and, from a technical point of view, the most complete, seen from near by, are but patches of color side by side, and only make an effect at a certain distance."

Vincent Van Gogh, November 1885

Conclusion

My goal has been to teach you how to make your own Quilted Photos. I hope you agree that I have reached my goal. I have prepared more Quilted Photography patterns for you on my website. To get them, come visit me at www.QuiltedPhoto.com. To get the additional patterns you will need the access code located in the lower right corner of page 77.

I have enjoyed sharing my ideas, and my quilts with you. I would also like to see your Quilted Photos. Please send me pictures of your projects.

Send your photos to:
Mosaic Quilt Studio
917 Fremont PMB138
South Pasadena, California, 91030

Thank you for your interest in "Simply Amazing Quilt Photography".

Tammie Bowser

"I am rich--not in money, but because I have found in my work something which I can devote myself to heart and soul, and which inspires me and gives meaning to life."

Vincent Van Gogh, March 1883

About The Author

I began sewing at four years of age. With my obvious natural talent for sewing I made my own clothing in jr. high and high school. I went on to fashion college (The Fashion Institute of Design and Merchandising). I studied fashion design, color theory and pattern making then graduated in 1985. My 17 year fashion career included positions as a fashion designer, production patternmaker and a first patternmaker.

I also studied website design, graphic design and desktop publishing. My computer knowledge combined perfectly with my design, fashion, and sewing knowledge. I went on to start a website called www.Ez-fit.com. This site made custom sized clothing patterns for people who sew.

Throughout my busy careers, I held an interest in quilting but, never took the time to learn it. With lots of time at home after my daughter was born, in the fall of 2000, I began to read books about quilting. Quilting captivated me, and I began to focus my creativity towards it.

I made my first quilt as a gift for my mother in November of 2000. I taught myself how to quilt by reading books, and watching the HGTV series, "Simply Quilts". After making that first quilt, I wanted to design my own quilt patterns. One morning just a few weeks later, I woke up with the idea for Quilted Photos. My first thought was that it couldn't work, but I made the first quilted photo that very week. I was amazed at how stunning the results were, and am still amazed every time I complete a Quilted Photo.

I think my career paths, and collection of knowledge has given me this unique approach to quilting. I hope you enjoy this innovative quilting style as much as I do.

Look for Tammie on HGTV's "Simply Quilts" episode #819

#559834h

"I have more ideas in my head than I could ever carry out....."

Vincent Van Gogh, May 1890

Quilted Photography Product Catalog

Light Fusible Interfacing

Fusible interfacing is a necessary item you will need to create your quilted photo. You will use it to fuse the fabric squares together before using the quick sewing technique (see chapter 3). The interfacing is used along with a grid guide. This interfacing has an adhesive that will hold your fabric squares firmly in place. The interfacing comes in 2 yard packages

Fabric Organizer

The best way that I have found to organize the fabric squares is to use this organizer case. It has 24 compartments of the perfect size. Look at chapter 2 to see just how important this simple tool is.

Distance Viewer

This is my favorite tool! This small scope will let you quickly see the photographic image in your quilt just by looking through it. It is useful while you are working on the quilt, and it is fun to use after the quilt is finished. Each time I work on a new quilt, I think to myself "It didn't work this time", when I look at the quilt through the distance viewer, the image just pops out at me! If you plan to make any of these quilts as gifts, you must give them a distance viewer too! You can get Distance Viewers at my website, www.QuiltedPhoto.com

Grid Guide

A grid guide is a full sized grid that is printed. The grid guide is placed under your fusible interfacing as a guide for placing your fabric squares. A grid guide can be used over and over to create quilted photos. You can even transfer the placement numbers onto the grid to make your quilted photo project easier to make. I have included a grid guide with this book, but you can re-order with the order form.

Get More Simply Amazing Quilted Photography !

Learn How To Make The Ultimate Scrap Quilt!

They are stunning to look at and amazingly easy to make! If you can sew a straight line, you can make your own in a weekend! Everyone who sees your quilted photography will think you are a genius!

It's as easy as 1-2-3!!

Rose Photograph

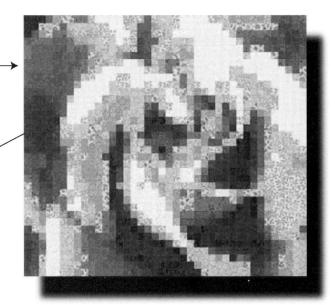

Close-up view of fabric